Photos de Voyage
A Gourmet's Journal

BILLY CONE

Edited by Nancy J. Jones, author of *Molly*

Pamela H. Quate Associates, Agent

Published By
HEXAGON BOOKS

P.O. Box 1284
Wrightsville Beach, North Carolina 28480
(910) 392-5063
ISBN 0-9704190-9-0

Library of Congress Control Number 00-134212

HEXAGON BOOKS

Printed in Wilmington, North Carolina
Wilmington Printing Company

E-mail: louiscone@aol.com
www.billyconephotography.com

ANOTHER BOOK BY BILLY CONE

Sixty Days Under The Influence
A Photo Journal Through France

INTRODUCTION

France is like an onion. Peal it and each layer reveals a different people of different means and backgrounds. But the two things that do not change from the outer skin to the core are their love for their language and good food. At the risk of sounding redundant, I cannot emphasize enough how much the French love to *bavarder* (converse) and to *bien bouffer* (eat well). Granted these things are important in corners all over the globe, but the French take them to a higher level of awareness and appreciation. If societies were judged by what their supermarkets sold, our brothers and sisters of the *Hexagone* would be the kings and queens of the planet. Further still, if civilization were judged by what the chefs in the most gastronomical of restaurants created, the French would be gods. Expats from all over the world, including America, have settled in this country for many reasons; however, the truth may be that they fell in love with the cuisine and the native tongue. It happens!

She is a woman, feminine yet in touch with her masculine side, seductive, artsy, full of history, and *chère* (expensive). She only demands of travelers some prior knowledge of her glorious past, a love of life, and plenty of *espèce* (cash). I call her *ma maîtresse* (my mistress), and for the last fifteen years she has been loyal as a companion and challenging as my teacher. If Heaven was a place, it would be on the Michelin Map of France.

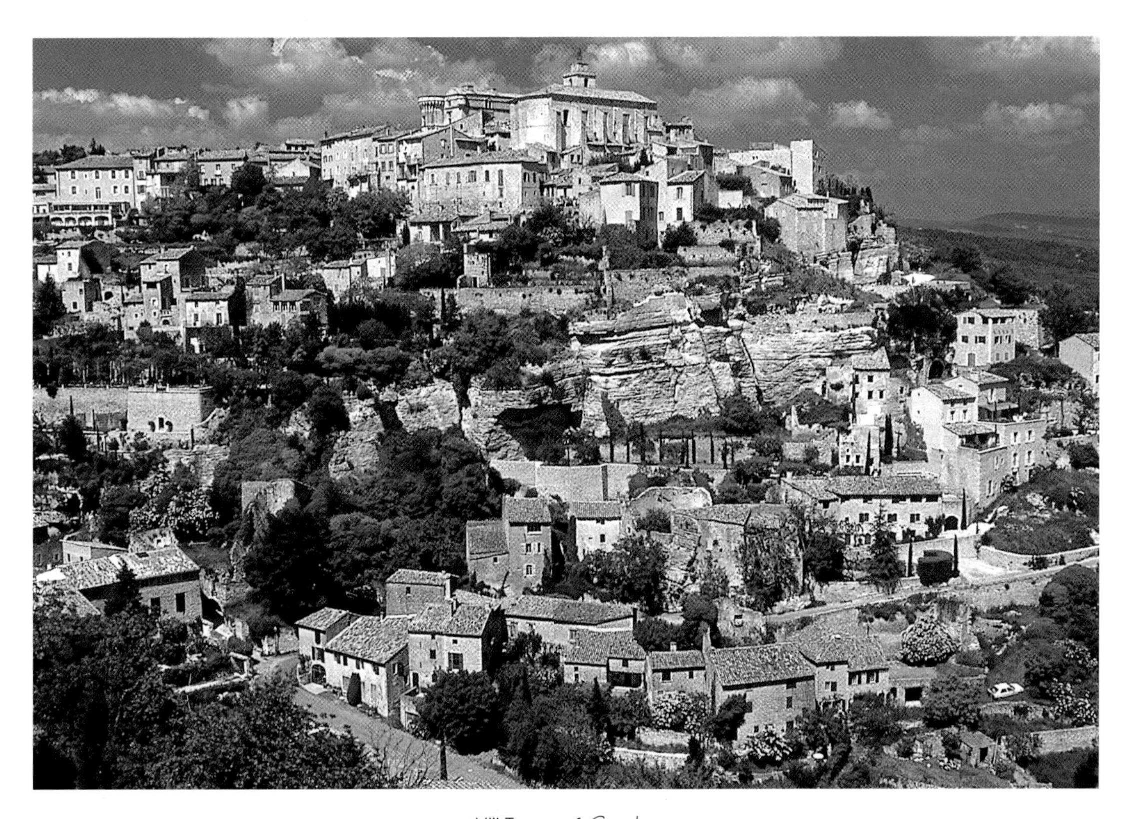

Hill Town of *Gordes*

France is one of if not the most *photogénique* countries in the world, and I am continually inspired by her inherent beauty. When you see something of aesthetic value all the time it can become almost banal; however, the geographical diversity of such a great nation keeps us photographers on our toes and tripods.

This journal is an exceptional photographic excursion through the heartland of *Gaul,* France's name when she was a Roman possession, with a large portion of time spent in the capital of light studying, shooting, eating, and dreaming. My account is personal and designed for you, the *lecteur* (reader), to live vicariously through me if you are so inclined. My writing is simple and describes the events of the day, tidbits about the country and its people, my feelings about things, and of course, the wonderful meals I was able to experience.

Mon séjour en France (my sojourn in France) took me from my studies at a language school and a stay with a centrally located French family in Paris to weekends with friends in *Nantes, Vichy, Lorient,* and the beautiful *Belle-Ile-En-Mer* on the Brittany coast. I traveled extensively in the famed region of *Provence* to the capital — *Aix-en-Provence* to many *anciens villages* (old villages) like the hill town of *Gordes*, the red clay cliff town of Roussillon, and the fabulous accommodations and cuisine of *L'Hôstellerie du Crillon-le-Brave,* looking out at some of *Cézanne's* favorite inspirations for paintings—*Mont Ventoux,* the *Plateau de Vaucluse,* and the Mountain of the *Lubéron*, and *ailleurs* (elsewhere). I flew to *Nice* and rented a car, visited *Menton* near the Italian *frontière* (border), drove the entire *Côte d'Azur* to the colorful fishing village of *Cassis*, saw *Marseille* through my lenses, stopped in *Saint Tropez*, visited friends in *Perpignan*, took an excursion with an English Lassie to *Cadeques* on the Spanish *Costa Brava*, and then spent five days in London so I could try out the new *Eurostar* speedtrain that practically flies through an underground underwater tube beneath the English Channel called the Chunnel to the French Capital in about three and a half hours, half the time it used to take by the older *moyens* (ways) of surface travel.

For all you photographers out there, my pictures are of the people, places and things which I found to be truly French; however some are Spanish and still others English. For each daily entry there is a photo, yet these entries are not designed to say much about the technical aspects of photographing a particular shot. Rather, the pix, as I call them, are to evoke an image of a country which likes to have its picture taken.

Amusez-vous bien (Enjoy)!

Friday the 12th and Saturday the 13th of April

My brother Steve and I dined on some real southern cooking on the way to New Hanover County Airport. We both ordered fried shrimp, veggies, hush puppies, and plenty of sweet iced tea. As usual, I was about forty-five minutes early. Steve carried one of my bags inside the airport, and we said good-bye.

In no time my plane touched down in Charlotte where I found out from a USAir representative that I might be able to ride the later non-stop flight to Philly instead of the one that lands in Raleigh. I chose not to gamble since this flight left after my original departure. We landed late in RDU and also in Philadelphia; however, there was plenty of time till my transatlantic voyage.

Aboard the Boeing 767, my neighbor and I discovered that the captain of this craft was a lady. A first for me but no worries! John was a rag salesman, and so we talked about textile machines (about which I knew zippo), about the city of Amsterdam (where he had business), and Cone Mills of Greensboro, North Carolina.

Dinner was definitely not of Air France quality, but the Glen Ellen cabernet sauvignon washed down the cheese raviolis, spinach, mixed greens, Monterey Jack and crackers quite well. Just like the meal, the flight was uneventful. And although that's not how I like my meals, it is how I like my flights.

Very thick clouds and fog socked in Paris, so all we could see during the final approach was, well, thick clouds and fog.

Corner *Café* at *rue de l'Eglise*

Just before the moment of contact with the shiny runway a busy highway came into view below and we were down. After going through customs and getting my bag without any delay, I caught a cab and proceeded to engage in the Parisian's favorite conversation — La chute de France (The Decline of France). Yes, according to our taxi man, France, and especially Paris, have been going downhill for the last fifteen years. "Without the tourists," he said, "Paris would be une ville morte (a dead city)." Oh, and how he complained about "La Grande Magique" (The Great Magic) of television! Apparently everyone just sits and watches the tube in their spare time now — A phenomenon originating in America which I call the Great Sedative or the Cheap Babysitter. Yes, America has come to France!

We stopped at #77 rue de l'Eglise (Church Street—every town has one). I punched the code and a buzzing sound let me into the building. Luckily, my French family lived on the Rez-de-chaussée (ground floor) of a rather modern appart (short for apartment). It would be very easy to come and go. Madame Besnier let me in and offered me a petit déjeuner of coffee and toast with butter. I declined but we chatted for a while, and I met Claire, one of her daughters. Then, as usual, I took a long walk to acquaint myself with the quartier—du quinzième (the fifteenth arrondissement). I soon discovered the local pâtisserie, the street corner café, and of course, the church in the very middle of it all. For school (language classes at the Institut de Langue Française) on Monday, I bought a notebook and a métro map.

Gee it was a chilly morning! To combat jet lag, I opted for a five hour nap, showered, walked some more, and took tea on the sidewalk of a small café. Then it was time to faire des courses (shop). At the nearby Franprix supermarché I picked up some bottles of mineral water, yogurt, and "Skip"(pronounced "skeep") laundry detergent. Note: If you are shopping for a lot of groceries one of those vinyl shopping carts that looks like a small rectangular golf bag on wheels seems to work well for many Parisians.

At "home" I unpacked my bags and had dinner—an excellent salad of endives, tomatoes, garlic, beans, and cucumbers in a lemon juice and walnut oil vinaigrette: steamed rice, and whole baked trout for le plat principal. After the meal, Claire and I watched La Grande Magique and I hit the sack around 21h30. Bonne nuit!

Paris, Sunday the 14th of April

I awoke around 8h15 and felt like a Mac truck had hit me in the night until I had my chocolat (hot chocolate) and yogurt. On this morn I walked to the Eiffel Tower, taking pictures along the way until I reached the Trocadéro, an expanse of two large rounding symmetrical buildings facing La Tour Eiffel with a kind of huge dance floor-like concrete platform in between for pedestrians leading to identical parallel cement sidewalks sandwiching fountains and modern sculpture. Very often, kids rollerskate and perform daring jumps for the passing tourists. Today however they must have still been au lit (in bed).

The twin buildings are now museums, and I especially wanted to see the work of Edward Baldus, a photographer in the 1800s who took pictures of cities, ruins, viaducts, et cétéra. Even more interesting to me was the other part of the Musée des Monuments Français that houses an incredible collection of various reproductions of parts of cathedrals from all over France. They looked so real, I thought they were somehow the originals, but then what would the cathedrals look like without their facades and gargoyles? And I thought I never made mistrakes!

After playing tourist, I walked down Avenue President Wilson to the Café Grand Corona. It was the prime time of day for cafés, however, no one was sitting outside YET—the sun was peaking through the thin veil of morning mist and the air was fresh and cool. People flock to the cafés when the sun comes out from its hiding place. I made myself comfortable somewhere in the middle of the sea of empty chairs. People would slow down, look at the vacant chairs and keep walking until

Espalande du Trocadéro

finally others began to find their perch for coffee, tea or hot chocolate, and for people watching. In Paris one must remember that a café is most often judged by who the clientele is and how many customers there are—this is why so often cafés go in and out of fashion here. The same can be said for restaurants, hotels, and of course, clothing.

La mode is everything in Paris. What was trendy six months ago may be all but forgotten next year. This is one reason why I believe that the French are the most educated and demanding consumers in the world. They are (from the upper crust to the blue collar family), intimately aware of the quality and choices available.

I waded through the crowd and ducked inside for a bite—simply a salade de crottin de chavignol chaud (baked goat's cheese salad on large croutons) and an Orangina. After lunch, I made my way up Avenue Montaigne to the foot of the Champs Elysées and proceeded to march up to the Virgin Megastore to buy Johnny Halladay's latest CD. To some, he's known as the French Elvis. To others, he's just a long blond-haired old man with bright blue eyes who sings American-style French rock and roll. I admire him for finding his niche in music and being successful. Look out! He's coming to America after thirty some years of gold records in French-speaking lands.

Métro home to put away my camera, and then a long walk to the famous literary café — Café de Flore, one of two great haunts for people watching, the other being Les Deux Magots just a block down Boulevard Saint-Germain towards Boulevard Saint Michel. I had a chilled glass of vin doux muscat (a rather sweet white wine perfect for an apéritif), and to go with the wine the waiter brought me a plate of green olives from Provence which is customary. Often in France a cocktail, whatever it may be, is accompanied by some kind of amuse-gueules (mouth teasers) like olives, nuts, popcorn, chips, or even wonderful baked chef's creations like miniature pâté en croute (country pâté wrapped in pastry).

My dinner at L'Arrosée, unlike last year, was except for the baked salmon in a citron vert (lime) cream sauce with noodles was not bad. The fish soup was a little tasteless and not cloudy at all, but the rouille (spicy mayo) was correcte (as it should be). The Bordeaux wine I drank was totally unacceptable, and I should have sent it back. That will be the last time I darken their doorway, even though the crème brulée is about the best I've had. Note: Restaurants are human. They can be incredibly good one time and outrageously bad the next. However, the difference is usually not that extreme, and I would say that usually the consistency of Parisian restos is rather good overall. Métro, Boulot, DoDo (Metro, Work, Sleep)!

Paris, Monday the 15th of April

Breakfast with Robert, another American locataire (boarder) and Madame's adopted son from Korea, Amori. We enjoyed the French favorite Banania brand hot chocolate, yogurt, and thin sliced baguettes with butter and jam. Very little dodo last night so I was dragging, however, I was early, and since the métro from Féix Faure to Etoile only takes 25 minutes I had a café on the way to class.

On this first day at the ILF (Institut de Langue Française) as with all students, I had to be placed in a course level matching my understanding of and fluency in French. What happened to me was that I found one of my earlier

Russian Church Near *Avenue Hoche*

professeurs, Michelle, who proceeded to grab me by the arm and physically put me in A2, the highest level at the school. Et c'est tout (And that's it)! I was pleased.

After class I was sort of led to take pictures of an interesting church located behind Avenue Hoche — an excellent subject to get my mind off of being tired. The sun made her features brilliant to the naked eye, alors, could I capture this on celluoid for the world to see? For lunch I ducked into the busy Hoche for an endive and roquefort salad and an Orangina. Quel plaisir (What a pleasure)! On a caffeine buzz, I continued on to the Parc Monceau to photograph the epitome of springtime in Paris—babies in strollers being pushed along the oval dirt path, benches presque complet (almost full), dogs on leashes, flowers blooming, the ciel Carolina blue, and green grass pushing up towards Heaven all around.

Around nine I met my friend Sheila at Café de Flore, the literary hangout of writers like Flaubert. After a glass of champagne complete with green olives from Provence we strolled over to Le Procope-the oldest restaurant in the world. The roasted scallops and pommes de terre (potatoes) were correcte (quite the way they were supposed to be), and a salade verte (green salad) was a nice complement to the rich seafood. For decadence we shared two chocoholics' delights—chocolate sorbet in a pool of firm milk chocolate with a truffle and an order of profiteroles au chocolat. Divine!

Sheila's from California, and she has lived in Paris as an expatriate for over thirteen years. We share a lot in common. One thing is that both of us had cars stollen in the capital city. Quels cauchmares (What nightmares)! More on that latter. Anyway, she told me an interesting tidbit.

When driving in Paris you should watch out for cars with CD (Corps Diplomatique) on the license plate because these folks are from Africa and are not the best drivers in the world. Sort of like the joke about the Belgians. Also, she told me that Paris is a woman! A demain!

The Original *Statue de la Liberté*

Paris, Wednesday the 17th of April

Bonne Anniversaire à Maman (Happy Birthday, Mom)! After class I metroed it to La Concorde where I continued à pied (on foot) to one of my favorite haunts—Angelina where you can sit for hours watching the crowd go by outside while you enjoy a tasty snack and beverage. I, being alone this day, had to have my chocolate fix of chocolat africain (thick puddin-like hot chocolate accompanied by fresh chantilly cream). Note: It is not a sin to return to your favorite places when visiting Gaul; besides we live in a small world.

Wrote several cartes postales to my family in the States on top of the beautiful round marble table top near the window of Angelina.

I find that I am at my creative best when traveling abroad. In France my burden is light. There's a wonderful feeling of freedom, having only my personal belongings and credit cards to worry about. Sometimes I feel a little irresponsible being single, self-employed, with no dependents, and footloose and fancy free in gai Pari. Most of the time I feel good about it 'cause Life's too short to worry about what you don't have! What a catharsis writing can be!

I walked back towards the Champs Elysées and the sun peaked through the French Impressionist clouds just enough to allow me some interesting people pix. A nice woman and her granddaughter made the shot of the day because it truly described what kind of day it was—beautiful and sunny. Along the lower part of the Champs before you get to all of the commerce, there are nice floral parks with benches

Grandmother and her *petite fille*

where Parisians love to sit and soak in the rays of soleil (sunshine). Home again on Bus #42.

Since Madame prefers that I not use her telephone, I make all of my calls for the day in the cabine téléphonique at the entrance to the métro Félix Faure. For calls in France I use a carte téléphonique of 120 or 50 unités, and for calls to the U.S. I use my MCI calling card. Today I talked to Anne-Sophie, Guy, Catherine, and Philippe who has organized a trip for us to Belle Ile-en-Mer the very day I will arrive in Paris on the Eurostar "Chunnel" Train from London. Oh yeah, in order to experience one of France's most celebrated technological advances—the Chunnel High Speed Train, I will have to travel to England for a few days. Stick with me. It will be fun I'm sure.

Dinner was served around nine and then I said to myself, "vas te coucher," which means in a lightly derogatory yet playful manner, "go to bed," of course I meant it in a nice way. Note: You can also say this to your dog or cat. À demain tout le monde (See you tomorrow everybody)!

Paris, Thursday the 18th of Avril

After several photographs of my friends who work at Le Hoche, I attended class. Within a matter of hours two people at school urged me to visit Les Jardins de Bagatelle (The Bagatelle Gardens) near Le Bois de Boulogne (The Boulogne Woods which is Paris' Central Park only not centrally located). The message was clear. From rue du Faubourg Saint-Honoré I took the #43 all the way across town past the well known district of Neuilly where many American Expats reside now, getting off near the Terminus (the last stop of a bus before it circles back in the opposite direction). After a short walk to the large gate I entered the walled-in area of what was more of a park than a garden. At first, what was heavily wooded led to gorgeous grassy open areas where le coq (a symbol of France—the rooster), le lapin (the rabbit), des cygnes (swans), and des canards (ducks) played among the flowers.

There, in the middle of all this was a painter with his easel set in the grass and a paintbrush in his hand. We struck up a conversation, and it turned out that he was un chomeur (an unemployed). He said he was living with his parents at the moment because he couldn't afford to support himself. I admired him for his spirit of creativity amidst what had to be personal turmoil. An engineer, the most prestigious profession in France, he was among many highly trained Frenchmen who were out of work. With his permission, I took his picture and continued on my way.

In class today I also discovered that Francis Cabrel was playing for the next three nights in a small venue called the Théâtre des Champs Elysées. So I got off the bus near Etoile and

La detente in the Bagatelle Gardens

while waiting for another, this respectable looking Iranian man showed me a notebook of horrendous atrocities that have occurred in his country in the recent past. I believed in his cause and helped him with cent francs. Was I a sucker? Maybe, but this man seemed so sincere, peaceful and genuine that I gave in. Finally my bus arrived, dropped me off near the métro, and je suis rentré (I went home).

Chez la famille (At the family's house), I changed clothes and headed to the theater to try to obtain a single ticket for the show. Of course they had sold out long ago, so I was prepared to get scalped. In my mind I believed I would be willing to pay 500 francs or $100. An hour before showtime, two rather large men began working opposite ends of the sidewalk looking to buy cheap and sell cher. I nervously walked back and forth and made my desire known to both men, but no one was selling. The pressure mounted. With fifteen minutes before the concert the Van Damm-like blond haired man made a purchase. I was on the scene like white on rice. 500 francs and it was mine. Yes! I was in.

I, probably coming from the farthest, wanting to see him the most, and certainly paying the dearest, got in at the horn. Je suis chanceux (I am lucky). From the front of the balcony I could see and hear quite well, and I was thrilled to be seeing my favorite singer after Reginald Dwight and Paul Hewson. Cabrel played almost all of his great songs, and I understood at least eighty percent of the words, because unlike even some English speaking singers, he sings quite clearly. After all, to me music carries a message, and if you cannot understand the lyrics you're sort of lost in the instrumental. Many times during the concert I got chills and even teary-eyed, because his songs are such a part of me now. We (the crowd) often sang along with Francis, and there were several standing ovations leading to brilliant encores.

Bus #80 to La Motte Piquet Grenelle, then the (M) home. Quelle merveilleuse journée (What a marvelous day)!

Paris, Vichy, Friday 19 avril

My current profs at the ILF (Institut de Langue Française) informed me today that come Monday, I will have all new teachers, just one of their practices to expose students to as many kinds of speakers as possible during their studies. Shoot! I was getting quite used to my conversation professeur. But that's the whole point in changing periodically—one must be able to comprehend a multitude of voices and speaking styles in order to become fluent in a foreign language. Je suis d'accord (I'm in agreement).

Métro home, but on the way I stopped in on this café/bar and had an excellent club sandwich on a baguette with homemade mayo. It was to die for! I enjoyed every bite and every sip of my Orangina outside in the beautiful French sunlight. Afterwards, I grabbed my things and headed for La Gare de Lyon where one catches trains heading south. What a long haul! First the Ⓜ to La Motte Piquet Grenelle, then Montparnasse Bienvenue, then Chatelet, and finally Direction Bois de Vincennes to the grande station. A cab might have made more sense.

Naturellement, I was early, allowing myself time to buy a ticket, a magazine, and a small bouteille d'eau—Vittel, one of Evian's competitors in France. Note: As a rule you must always composter (have your ticket punched in one of the many orange machines found near the voies or quais (tracks) to validate the ticket for the day's date). If you forget you will have to pay again plus a fine inside the train. Et oui (Yep)! C'est comme ça (It's like that)! Also note: Get on the train that stops at your city even though its final destination may be further along. In my case I got on the train that was

Stacking the *Métro*, *Café*, and *Pâtisserie*

going to the town of Clermont Férrand, forty minutes further down the line from my destination—Vichy. Note also: Since I did not reserve my billet (ticket) twenty-four hours in advance, I had to find a non-fumeur (non- smoking) wagon where the seat wasn't reservé. I staked my claim, turned on Peter Gabriel's "So", and we were rolling.

Michel [my friend Evelyne's petit ami (boyfriend)] arrived and we immediatement began to kid each other sarcastically. We joked and fooled each other until we got to a special patisserie where they often buy the specialty of the region—pâté de pommes (potato pâté). We also bought some sinful desserts. Then we had drinks at L'Autre Source, a wine bar par excellence. Michel had beer while I sipped Kir Royals, but I wasn't expecting him to pay for them. Oh well! My man, Francis Cabrel had just given a concert in Vichy days earlier, and there was an awesome autographed poster of him on the cold box. One day I'll get one like it! So cool!

At the house in Cusset (Vichy's sister city) Evelyne had just arrived from work. She looked well. Around 21h30 we sat down to dinner and more wine. We ate a salade mixte, pâté de pommes, an assortiment de fromages (cheeses), almond tarts, and chocolate delights. After the simple meal the sofabed was mine, and I hit it hard. Bonne nuit!

Vichyssois imitating Michael Jordan

Vichy, samedi 20 avril

Warm and beautiful day in Cusset! Took pix around the house and helped with the barbeque while listening to Francis Cabrel's "Fragile" album. Who could ask for more? Last night I played some of my crazy compositions on Evelyne's piano, and she said that she enjoyed them. Today she told me that she was writing an article about me in La Montagne, a regional newspaper. How exciting can you get! To accompany this article she took a picture of me outside her house as I was taking a picture of some flowers. What a joy and a pleasure it is when someone takes an active interest in you as a person! When the story comes out Evelyne will send me a copy. So cool! Of course it will be en français, so only a few of my friends in America will be able to decipher it.

In the nearby town of Vichy I found myself wandering around the Mairie (Town Hall) and came upon two boys playing. They couldn't believe I was a real American right there in their little town. We talked and I asked if I could take their pictures. One boy said he would do an imitation of Michael Jordan, tongue out and all. I'd say he did a good job of it.

Le chien (the dog), a long-haired German Shepherd, s'appelle (is called) Domi, and he doesn't like me. He doesn't like strangers at all. I hate dogs like that. And is it true that dogs take on the personality of their masters? Probably! It's Michel's. No comment.

Warm winds caressed our sparsely clothed bodies on the terrace as we enjoyed grilled pork chops, thin French green beans in butter, and a salade. Et bien sur, du vin rouge. The weather was nice and the temperature was over 55 degrees

Fahrenheit—sweater weather quoi! Quoi means "what", but in this case it is almost non-translatable. It could mean, "you know?" or "or what?".

Around 17h00 (5:00—always subtract 12 from the time above 12 and you get the PM time) Evelyne and I arrived in Vichy chez (at the home of) Madame Bonnefoy, and she was as spirited as ever. We all sipped glasses of sparkling wine and caught up a bit. At the time she was lodging two Koreans who were attending the local language school—CAVILAM. In one week Madame would be off to her condo in Spain. Ah, la vie française (Oh the French life)!

Upon returning to Cusset, I showed Evelyne and Michel my small portfolio of slides which I just happened to have because I am supposed to do a show in Paris in a restaurant/gallery in September of this year. Boy, was I psyched about that! Just think who might see my photography in the City of Light.

That evening I took my hosts to dinner at a nearby chateau called the Theillat (an old estate with 18 rooms, a pool, and of course, un bon restaurant), and we dined royally. I had Kir Royals, mouth teasers, warm langoustine salad, Tournados Rossini in a rich brown sauce with mushrooms and foie gras on top. Before taking dessert, we were graced by a tart green apple sorbet with Calvados to cleanse the palate. Excellente! I tasted their desserts, but ordered none for myself—very American thing to do! After a trip to la toilette, I asked the owner/chef if I could acquire one of his beautiful Laurent Perrier ashtrays (I collect ashtrays with names of alcoholic beverages or cigarettes which are now illegal to manufacture in France.), and on my way out he offered it to me as a cadeau. Incroyable! Merci beaucoup et à bientôt (Thank you and see you soon)!

Vichy

Vichy, dimanche 21 avril

Around 11h00 we had le petit déjeuner together—coffee and apple pear tart made by my hostess. Then they took me to a place high on a hill overlooking all the little towns called, "Les Hauts de Hurlevent." A huge television and radio tower stands on top of this mount, and strong winds can often be heard blasting past this metal structure in the sky. People were flying kites and picnicking in the grassy area all around. Of course, I was busy shooting all of this and taking it all into my memory. You could see Vichy in the distance down in the valley from such a vantage point. I just imagined the impressionist painters having a field day there with the colorful kites, the people, and the view.

We returned chez Evelyne and ate lunch outside in the sunshine—I can't believe this gorgeous weather! Le déjeuner? Oblong red and white bite-size radishes with butter and salt, quiche with potatoes and ham, salad with endives, fraises avec sucre et crème fraîche (strawberries with sugar and fresh cream), and more glasses of Beaujolais than anyone needs for lunch, but, hey, we're in France where tout est possible (The French often like to say this. It means "anything is possible").

Before my departure I went back to Vichy for some last minute pix, and I really liked the one of the church and colorful pink building.

Au revoir Vichy, Cusset, et mes amis! Uneventful three hour jaunt to Paris, a short wait in a long line for a cab, a long ride across town, and many letters waiting for me at home. I love to get mail, especially handwritten personal stuff. Before savoring mon courrier (mail) I made calls in what has become my personal cabine téléphonique. I called Thierry, Jeanne-Mairie, Anne-Sophie, Guy, and my artist friend Cécile who had just phoned from Nantes. I'm invited to her home the third of May. J'attends avec impatience (I can't wait)!

The ideal place to be in Paris when you are alone is either au musée (at a museum) ou au café (or at a coffee shop), and I needed a convenient place to read my letters and have a beer, so I hit the nearby corner caf. These were not ordinary letters! They were bound in handmade paper covered in exotic designs wrapped in color—matching bows. What a creative spirit that fashioned these! Most people have forgotten how to write letters in this day of the widespread "stick in thumb pull-out-plum" mentality. Just call me! Calling is so easy. I enjoy letters, because they take thought and inspired imagination both to write and to read. These were excellent. I felt good as I sipped my beer and read. Alone? Are you kidding?

Amori, the thirteen-year-old Korean boy and I shot the bull for a while before I went to my room to write. I couldn't wait to tell some of my friends how I got to see Francis Cabrel. Skipped dinner—probably a sin in France. Ate too much this weekend! Salut!

Paris, lundi 22 avril

At school I discovered that I really like my new teachers, both women, extra nice, and bright. Over the years, I've found that the most creative teachers are the best, because with their novel approaches, they know how to get students involved in conversation about n'importe quoi (anything). This is truly the case at the ILF.

Afterwards, I ducked into a local sunlit café and lunched on a Spécialité d'Auvergne (a specialty from the region of Auvergne where Vichy is found)—petit salé (salty pork on the bone or off with lots of fat), lentils, une salade verte (a green salad), and an Orangina. L'addition (the bill) was just over $20. Pas mal (not bad)!

This après-midi (afternoon) I had to run some errands to the FNAC for the newly released Clannad tape and then on to La Poste for one of their folded boxes and some timbres (stamps). On the way home in the subway I had the great idea to take my "traveling companion" to the top of the Tour Montparnasse to get a few pix of Paris from above. Although the air was clear on high, below it was a bit brumeux (hazy). No worries! I shot a roll anyway just for fun. Besides, there are so many recognizable sites to see from up there, even in the brume. Of course there is the Seine, the church of St. Germain, the Luxembourg Gardens, St. Sulpice, Rue de Rennes, cemeteries, football (soccer) fields, and La Gare Montparnasse where I had to go next to buy my train tickets for my upcoming weekends in Nantes and Lorient.

At the station Bus #95 was waiting for me, so I got on and rode to the Opéra Garnier (the Academy of Music in the first arrondissement) where I took a few clichés (photographs)

View from the top of *La Tour Montparnasse*

before being transported to Ⓜ Cluny in Bus #21 where I got carded without a photo by the "men in green" (transportation officials who check for invalid tickets). My "carte hebdomodaire" (weekly transportation pass) requires a personal photo, alors (welp), leave it to a photographer not to have one. Since this was my second warning, I figured I better get the picture. Get it?

Je suis rentré (I went home) to relax, shower, and write. My blind date arrived in her Golf (a popular car in France because its not too small, its not too expensive, and it flys), and we stopped at Oh Poivrier! for exotic drinks and awesome smoked salmon on buttered Pôilane toast. The best! Then we traversed the river and dined outside this cute little place called, La Rose de France, open near the métro Pont Neuf since 1966. Anne-Sophie had boudin blanc (white blood sausage) with baked apples, both of which I tried. But I truly enjoyed the Coquilles Saint Jacques on a bed of leeks in a cream sauce. Extra (very good)!

I should have picked the wine; however, because her selection of a Sancerre may have been "correcte" in a traditional sense, but a light red would have refreshed the palette more. Note: A white has to be exceptional for me to appreciate it. Wine was meant to be red. What can I say? Besides, Jesus' blood is red. Right! Only I, the gourmand side of me, had the glace (ice cream) with Macedoine de fruits in alcohol, hot chocolate sauce, and chantilly. After her décaf we drove around the enlightened city and she took me home where Amori, Madame, and I visited for a while. Never a dull moment! Á demain!

Paris, mardi 23 avril

Le matin comme d'habitude (The usual morning of class et cétéra). For le déjeuner I opted for something rapide at the chain of Italian restos called Pizza Vesuvio. The tagliatelli carbonara was correcte but not stupendous, and it came with a simple insalata verde (green salad). People who visit the capital but who have never lived here for any length of time will tell you to avoid the chain restaurants. I've found that these places often have plats du jour (daily menu specials) at a prix intéréssant, alors, for a simple lunch this suits me just fine when I'm not trying to impress anyone.

Afterwards I took some pix around Les Champs Elysées (the Elysée Fields turned concrete jungle, but somehow pleasing because of all the tree lined sidewalks, pedestrians, restaurants, and shops), but the overcast skies were threatening, so I took Bus #43 home. Later I took the #82 to the Jardins du Luxembourg (Luxembourg Gardens), and just as we approached the Terminus (the end of the line) drops of French water began splattering the bus's windshield. Merde!

I stayed on the bus and rode till we reached the Café Sufferen, where I indulged in tea and sugar with milk as I wrote some cartes postales. Overhearing conversations in restos and cafés is a common occurrence in big cities, but I was trying hard not to listen to the couple next to me. They must have thought I was just a dumb tourist with a fancy camera, because they proceeded to speak so loud that I couldn't help but hear. Wow! You don't say! They were talking about the third member of a love triangle—

Beautiful Face Preserved in Bronze

apparently a single woman. The two of them were married it seems, but after I left the caf I thought that they could have staged the whole thing for laughs. But that would not be French. All that for who, me? Hardly! It is appropriate here to mention again that the French often love to say, "Tout est possible" (Everything is possible)!

The rain subsided, allowing me to walk home relatively dry for dinner which was not very memorable. In bed I listened to Enya while I studied and read until I couldn't keep mes yeux open. Bons rêves (Sweet dreams)!

Paris, mercredi 24 avril

This morning it took two crèmes (café au lait) to get me going to school, where we worked on my least favorite verb tense (one that is only used in writing, never spoken)—le passé simple. The simple past is not so simple. But if you read a lot of great French literature, you should be intimately familiar with its conjugations point à la ligne (period). Personally, I get by. I can at least recognize the tense when I encounter it.

Uri, my Russian friend, and Sophie, une anglaise (a Brit) are the most interesting people in class, because they talk a lot and show an interest in the other students. Note: The key to learning a foreign language is to speak up and say what you can whenever you can. This requires you to take an active interest in everyone and everything around you. There is little room here for the meek and timid; however, they too can learn in private, but it's out in the world where we must operate.

Lunch at the Bistro Roman—tomatoes and mozzarella salad, margret de canard au poivre vert (sliced roast duck breast with green peppercorn sauce), all the French fries I could eat, and a Coke, Vintage 1997. Oh, and of course, lots of Ketchup.

Jean-Baptiste Camille Corot, a great French painter who lived during the first three quarters of the nineteenth siècle (century) and who painted marvelously till he was in his late seventies, was being exhibited at the Grand Palais (a museum called the Grand Palace), so I bought my ticket and entered his world. He painted many landscapes especially in Rome and other regions of Italy. He painted

Saint-Sulpice Church

large mythical and Biblical scenes as well as portraits. In his oeuvres (works) he translated the subtle values of light and atmospheric conditions, preparing the way for the grandest artistic movement—Impressionisme. I loved the exhibit!

Once again, I took #82 to Les Jardins de Luxembourg, yet this time pas de pluie (no rain). I shot people all afternoon. It was great! The soleil was shining, humanity was out in numbers, and no one cared if I took their picture. Around the pond, where all the children play with wooden sailboats, was the best place.

As the day wore on, I made my way to the great church of Saint-Sulpice and photographed the fountain and the grand edifice. I also stopped to take tea just outside the church. What's so nice about working in Paris is that there are so many distractions and cafés that you are unaware of ever getting anything done. It's great!

At eight I punched the code at 20, avenue de l'Opéra, and Guy invited me in for a drink. Then we had an excellent dinner at Le Grand Colbert—grilled lamb steak cooked in garlic and parsley, pommes de terre dauphinoises (garlic and cream potatoes), profiteroles au chocolat, and décaf. We talked about my life, the book, my family, and his work, without fail his work. C'est tout (That's it)! Métro, dodo!

Paris, jeudi 25 avril

Métro to Ledru Rollin where I called my mysterious pen pal in the States. It's like I have a petite amie (girlfriend), but I don't even know her yet. Her letters are much more romantic than calling her at eight o'clock in the morning EST.

Lunch time! Nearby I found an excellent Chinese resto and wolfed down the following: Nems (a kind of eggroll without the egg and flour made with rice paper instead that you wrap into mint and lettuce leaves and dip in a sweet vinaigrette—a must when dining on la cuisine chinoise), du porc aigre-douce (sweet and sour pork), riz (rice), and a glass of rosé which goes well with food from the Orient. Note: Drinking a couple of glasses of beer or a half carafe of wine for lunch is no biggie here even for businessmen.

My next destination was the Viaduc des Arts, an old railroad viaduct, the lower part of which has been converted into ateliers/magasins (workshops/stores) that sell what else—ART. The upper level, where the trains used to pass, is now the Promenade Plantée (a nice walking path with all varieties of plant on both sides of where the tracks used to be. Not something to do on a short visit to Lutèce; however, if you spend a lengthy time there, go! What I really admire is that the French don't just tear old edifices down and build heartless modern eyesores for the voiceless next generation. They preserve their precious past.

Walking! This is the way most Parisians get to and fro, and they are lucky, because they get to see a beautiful city everyday with everchanging humanity all about. In essence, they are in this huge unfeeling world, yet they get to see that they are not alone. La foule (the crowd) is energizing.

Viaduc des Arts With *La Promenade Plantée* Above

Walking is also energizing, not to mention good exercise in a lifestyle that may not allow for daily workouts at the gym. Besides, there are not many places to workout even in Paris. The health craze is coming but it's not here yet. Thank God!

Speaking of health, I downed a Kir Royal (champagne and Crème de Cassis). Santé (To your health)! Then I punched the code at Emory's on the rue de Rivoli, where I watched him and his black lab cook dinner for ten. We dined royally on rare sliced duck breast, hash browns, string beans, and a salad. The food was quite good, but the wine which came from Emory's family winery was the treat of the evening. In all, we drank kirs, white wine, red wine, champagne, and hard cider. Fortunately, one of Thierry's teetotaling friends gave me a ride home. Salut (Ciao)!

Paris, vendredi 26 avril

I'm past the stage when school wracks my brain. Hallelujah! My level of fluency allows me to concentrate on what I don't understand, and that has become less and less. Le Journal (News) still gives me a fit though. Guess it always will!

Amori borrowed his Mom's camera, and together we went to find a lithium battery for it. We were lucky. The first photo shop we encountered had just what we needed, so off we went to Le Jardin de Luxembourg for some fun. Although he had never taken pictures before, he was game. He watched me for a while before taking his first pix. Once he saw what pleased him, he overcame his gunshyness. We walked over to the beautiful Panthéon, a monument built on the mount of Sainte-Geneviève in the cinquième (5th arrondissement) around 1764 by a man named Soufflot. How boring! I'm just kidding, but aren't you glad I'm not giving you all the dates and names of who built this and who painted that? Today it is the resting place for great French historical figures—lately there has been a great deal of fuss and excitement over one of its latest permanently enshrined guests, Andre Malraux, an early twentieth century writer and homme politique (politician) who wrote about overcoming the corruptions of the day.

When we were in the Luxembourg Gardens I took a picture of a statue of a dancer with flowers around it and the Panthéon in the background. I used my fill flash to illuminate the statue and the flowers because we were in the shade.

On the way home in the bus I noticed that my lens cap was missing. Being a perfectionist, I freaked. Where in Paris would I find another? I began to search my pockets.

Luxembourg Gardens and *Panthéon*

Of the six possible pockets I was only considering five, and I was so lucky once again. It was in the sixth and least likely one. The trials of a photographer!

Home to relax, and have dinner. What I was served looked like pigs feet, but apparently they were parts of turkey thighs or something like that. They actually went well with the leeks and potatoes, but the acid tap water left a bit to be desired. Et oui (Yep)! Even in the heart of the capital of cuisine l'eau du robinet (the tap water) is full of fluoride and chlorine like America's. No wonder everybody is lugging large plastic bottles of precious clear liquide around everywhere you go! And no wonder there is a bottle of it on every restaurant table in France! Tap water is potable (drinkable) by God, but I'd only shower in it. À demain!

Paris, samedi 27 avril

Grasse Matinée (I slept in) and took my grand crème (espresso with milk) at a crowded café not far from my destination—Le Dôme Des Invalides. I took photos of a man flying his high-tech kite made in California on the lawn in front of L'Ecole Militaire (The Military School) and then walked through the Invalides to photograph the freshly cleaned stone building of Le Dôme.

Quelle belle journée (What a beautiful day)! Too bad I was too pressé (in a hurry) to walk and had to go underground! Where was I going? Place de Clichy, not far from the Cimetière de Montmartre, a cemetery that began to turn my stomach from all the graves and tombs, flowers and stones. A beloved French singer, Dalida, was there, and I shot her tombeau (tomb). Then I worked my way up the Butte de Montmartre to the Place des Tertres and the Sacré Coeur basilica. These are beautiful places to see in The City of Light, but as is often the case, there were too many people meandering around. Gee, everywhere I went was crowded today! I had to métro it home to regroup.

William Hurt and a wonderful French actrice were starring in a film called "Un Divan À New York", so I decided to find a theater playing it. It was so clever! A French lady comes to New York City and takes over Hurt's counseling practice by accident, and Hurt goes to her dumpy appart in Paris. Both French and English are spoken, and the ending is drôle (funny). William Hurt speaking French was the best part.

With time to kill, I sat down in a popular café and just soaked it all in. It was a beautiful scene—all the tables

Le Dôme des Invalides

outside with their colorful umbrellas were full of people listening to the music of an accordion player with the rushing traffic behind, the tall Spring green trees lining the quai lit up by the bright white light coming from a bateau mouche cruising the Seine below, and the wind blowing violet petals like snow over the whole scene. Only in Paris! After writing a few post cards and downing my beer, I met my friend Lynn and a friend of hers at the Hotel Colbert near the quartier latin. We walked and talked and they filled me in on the theft of all of their belongings in the town of Chinon. Poor guys! They had to buy all new clothes in Angiers. Luckily, they had their money and passports on them at the time the bags were stolen.

We dined at Le Procope and were not disappointed—endive and roquefort salad, grilled sole, filet mignon with béarnaise sauce, cauliflower au gratin, green beans, braised tomatoes with spices, creamy garlic potatoes, Croze Hermitage Burgundy, and sorbet au chocolat sur une nage de chocolat et sa truffe. Note: Only one out of four taxi drivers would admit that they knew where the nearby Colbert was because they don't like what is called "petites courses" (less profitable short rides).

Paris, dimanche 28 avril

Café au lait at another nearby yet further café than the day before. Writing and watching all that happens on a Sunday in front of the church. At noon, the bells sound, people slowly exit, not all dressed up like in the States. Old folks walk past me, and a gypsy girl comes up to my table for a handout. I give her a dollar's worth of francs, and she comes back later with a half-eaten apple. She asks me for water but leaves before I can slip her cent francs ($20). La vie est dure (Life is hard)! People disappear from outside the café. It's only me and a woman who seems alone. She looks for companionship in her magazine and tea, but she knows it will not endure. The sole of her shoe is coming apart at the seams, and her nails are bitten to the quick. She is very calm. Her auburn hair is clean, shining in the milky light. Almost a quarter to one and we are the only souls outside this establishment. She is not having a five course lunch with friends and family today like most Parisians. Today she might skip lunch altogether and enjoy her solitude. She is with herself today. And me, well, I've got my writing and a book and we are not much different. The bells toll again and life goes on in the heart of Paris.

Enough seriousness! Off to the Champs for an all American lunch at the newly opened Planet Hollywood—excellent club sandwich, fries, and a Coke. Just like home, I thought—so relaxing and pleasant to be served there by young, friendly, and bilingual waitpeople while enjoying the music and TV monitors showing recent Hollywood hits. For English speaking tourists and curious Frenchmen, Planet Hollywood is an oasis of Americana. I took my coffee at the elaborately modern bar counter, and after a song by Wang Chung, I split.

L'Eglise Near My French Family's House

Most French restaurants seem to be so regimented and conditioned by tradition. For example, you are often expected to begin with an apéritif (cocktail) then an entrée (appetizer), next a plat principal (main course), rarely but sometimes another plat, wine of course, dessert, and café. If you skip any of these it may take the waiter out of his precious rhythm. I even left out the cheese and fruit courses that sometimes accompany the meal. Don't get me wrong. I like to eat like a king, but not always. I've also noticed that French restos don't have enough waitpeople to serve a full house. They are often running themselves ragged. Note: Usually there are one or two seatings per meal and the restaurants fill up all at once. If you come before or after the crowd then you will be out of sync, out of the natural rhythm of the waiters. In this case, your food may take much longer, and you will constantly need to ask your server for something, irritating yourself and waiters around you.

In contrast to my meal, I saw a movie that was cent pourcent (100 percent) français—Desiré, staring Jean Paul Belmondo. Malheureusement (Unfortunately) there was so much slang that I couldn't enjoy the film. Note: Most films in the first eight arrondissements are VO (Version Originale), usually in English or French with no subtitles. Outside of this part of the "snail" (system of sections of Paris which looks like an escargot), the VO films have subtitles or are dubbed in French and the VF (Version Française) films are all French or with French subtitles.

After a few photos, I took the métro home and ate dinner at a Thai restaurant called Chanthaboury on rue Beaugrenelle. Excellent soup and satay with a delicious sauce and a cocktail maison with a lèché fruit in it. C'est tout (That's it)!

Paris, lundi 29 avril

Once you get your carte orange (weekly or monthly transportation pass) and a passport-type photo then all you need each time you renew is the little yellow ticket which slides into a plastic pocket in the pass. This ticket will slide through the machines at every métro and on every bus, hopefully never being eaten. My carte cost 67 francs which amounts to about thirteen dollars. Not bad, seeing how an average taxi ride with pourboir (tip) will cost just a little less than the total cost of the pass.

I hit the Hoche hard for a grand crème so I could stay awake in class. Based on fifteen years of studying in French language schools, I have noticed a bias towards controversial

Lovers *Sur La Quai De La Seine*

subjects in conversation classes. The French like to argue. It's like a sport here. And what better way to stimulate speaking than with a heated topic? Today was no exception. My conversation group talked about the difference between "guilty" and "responsible". Note: This has absolutely nothing to do with OJ who is almost unknown here in Europe. Lately we have been discussing whether individuals who are outcasts from society (les marges de la société) should be considered responsible for the bad they perpetrate. Stimulating stuff!

Another crème at the Hoche prepared me for two more hours of concentration, only this time it was dictation with pas mal (quite a bit) of passé simple. For lunch I dined on a chicken, lettuce, tomato, and mayo baguette sandwich and a Coke from the French version of a fast food sandwicherie—Pomme de Pain.

Caught the #42 home and set out to photograph L'Hôtel de Ville. No, not a hotel or the name of a new Cadillac, but a beautiful old building on the Left Bank where the mayor of Paris lives and works. I walked around Notre-Dame and caught some lovers near the Ile Saint-Louis. Sneaky people pictures! Guilty but not responsible! Rode the #72 to Alma Marceau where I took #42 home for dinner—salad and chicken and rice with sweet and sour sauce.

Saw the film "Mary Reilly" (really Dr. Jeckl and Mr. Hyde) at Gaumont Montparnasse, and thought that John Malkovic, Julia Roberts, and Glen Close were excellent. When the Doctor said that he "had a tear in the seam of his soul and that he had the taste of oblivion," I myself felt I could relate. Guilty or responsible again? Walking home, the moon and the stars shown brightly, and I thought to myself, this must be some kind of record for consecutive beautiful days in Paris. Bons rêves (sweet dreams)!

Bread Lady In A *Boulangerie*

Paris, mardi 30 avril

Montana is born! Yes, another of my precious nephews has arrived. Here's to his long and happy life on earth. Who knows, he may live part of his life on another planet.

Class was good—encore des nuances (more nuances). This is an important word, because for every rule in French there are exceptions or nuances which drive students of the language crazy. Like me! My theory is that the French have never wanted foreigners who have not been properly tried, tested, initiated, and assimilated into their culture to be mistaken for "real" Frenchmen. No, but it's true! There are idioms known only by Frenchmen, and if you cannot speak this tongue then you can't capture the flag so to speak. You will always be unFrench. There is hardly a melting pot in this country. It's kind of like a club having passwords to keep those who don't belong (yet) where they belong—outside. But hey, ask anyone, it has backfired on them, because even the French often make little mistakes with the language.

Enjoyed lunch at the popular Le Matignon near the Lancel store au bas des Champs Elysées (at the bottom of the Elysian Fields). A nice American couple in their sixties sat next to me, and they told me they were staying at one of the world's finest and most expensive addresses—L'Hôtel de Crillon. Last night they dined at one of the world's most expensive restaurants—Laurent. They laughed and told me they were "blowing their kid's inheritance" for his sixtieth birthday. Funny! I had lotte roti (long round silver flaky white meat fish) with ratatouille and a glass of red. For them, this was like eating fast food. "Blowing their kid's inheritance!" I love that one!

Later, at home, I boxed up my CD's and collection of ashtrays et cétéra and took them down to La Poste where it cost me un bras et une jambe to send the package par avion (220 francs or $44). Autoroute robbery!

I took my camera on a wild goose chase in buses looking for the sun and any interesting subject I haven't already seen here. Unfortunately it was an act of futility. Pas de soleil (no sunshine)! But I did use my flash at the Hôtel Crillon itself when the two doormen allowed me to take their picture. Later I ended up at my favorite salon de thé called Ladurée for some hot Ceylan Devonian tea with milk and a pistachio macaroon with lots of pistachio flavored butter cream inside. Now that is a sweet! Note: This is an excellent place to relax with a friend or lover, write a postcard, and above all, people watch.

Going to Paris without the desire to shop is like going to bed without the desire to, well, sleep. Everybody who comes here does it. It doesn't mean you have to buy anything, although that is also quite fun. Today, for example, I bought a marron (autumn brown) Yves Saint-Laurent button down and a (black) linen T-shirt noire, two things I couldn't buy much less find at home. Note: Very rarely can you find a deal on French goods sold in the States; therefore, if you can get them on a jaunt to New York, Chicago, LA, or even in your home town, then wait till you get home to buy it. Of course there are exceptions to every silly rule. You're here to enjoy yourself, so go for it. Besides, when they ask you where you got that you can say—"oh... FRANCE!"

By the way, I always carry my camera even when I shop. A very nice lady who sells wonderful breads in a boulangerie let me take her picture. Not everyone in this country is too into themselves to be friendly. However, a few bad apples can spoil the whole bunch, sometimes even in my own country.

Speaking of home, I went to my temporary home away from home and had a simple dinner—radishes with butter and salt, spicy sausages called merguez, and powdered mashed potatoes. Et oui, même en France (Yep, even in France)! Après le dîner (after dinner), I went to a bar called the Cosmos near Montparnasse, and listened to old disco tunes of the '70s and '80s, drank an exotic $12 drink with two inches of foam on top, breathed in a lot of smoke, wrote several postcards, and met no one. Don't let anyone fool you! It ain't easy to meet Parisians or French people for that matter. Nine times out of ten a foreigner's best friends in Paris will not be French. Asian, Italian, German, Dutch, American but not Parisian. That's just the way it is here. The average Frenchman or woman is next to impossible to befriend much less meet at a bar. Slow métro for dodo. Salut!

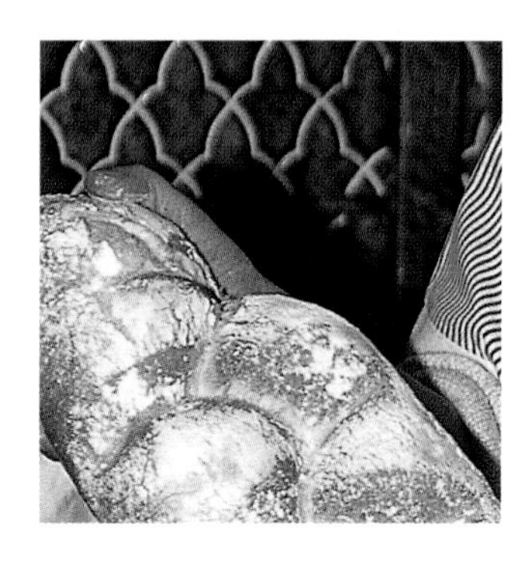

Street Artist And His *Création*

Paris, mercredi 1 mai

Labor Day (International Workers Holiday) for the French! Everything's supposed to be closed. And what would you know, on my way out with my "traveling companion" under cloudy skies I stumbled upon this fabulous little Italo-Franco restaurant and had a most memorable meal. After two half bottles of Valpolicella produced glass bits on the rims of the bottles, the owner brought me an excellent Chianti Classico which of course cost more, but was well worth it. Then came the bruchetta amuse-gueules *(mouth teasers) which were almost as good as Mom's and she's not even Italian. Next, I had grilled* polenta *with mushrooms sautéed in fresh garlic and* huile d'olive *(olive oil) on arugula. Stupendous!*

The room temperature red went perfectly with my next course—an authentic risotto Milanese. Ah, saffron! Gee, I have expensive taste! I really needed to speak Italian but didn't want to bother the chef, so I remained quiet and ate the most authentic Italo-Franco Tiramisu and caffe I've ever had. Quel repas (What a meal)!

Although the heart of the Heavens can be difficult to find at times, I set out to find the sun with very little luck. Comme d'habitude (As usual), I walked and walked, but the shots were just not there or had I just eaten myself into oblivion? Whatever the case may have been, I wasn't seeing anything of aesthetic value or pleasure until I ran across a street artist who had painted two lovely pastels on the sidewalk. I was so impressed that I took his picture along with his art. Note: Paris is such a civilized city that sidewalks are large and wide so even street artists can perform for the crowds that happen by. I took the #80 home. In the café du coin (corner café) a cute little chien (dog) came up to me and I gave him a sugar cube to suck on. He liked it. Then another dog on a leash wanted in on the action right there in the café. Only in France! Also only in France are people selling muguets (Lilys of the valley) on every other street corner this Labor Day seulement (only). They truly smell sweet like some precious nectar of the gods.

For dinner we had poupette de veau (veal in a round bird-like parcel tied with string) with mushrooms, carrots, parsley and potatoes. Quite good actually! I wrote myself to sleep.

La Poste

Paris, jeudi 2 mai

Two crèmes (pronounced crim) and class. We talked about the Latin Spirit in the world today and what it means. Stereotypes abound! But it was very interesting. He's the great lover, the hot temper, the jealous one, the artist, the gourmet and the list goes on.

The Latin Spirit in me came out at Au Bon Accueil (The Good Greeting) for a lunch that was quite simply sublime. First I had a salad with a round of warm Saint-Marcellin cheese on top. Wow, that is the creamiest cheese with the richest flavor I've ever tasted! Un verre du Chinon to go along with the Méli-Mélo (mixed grill of fish filets) in a delectable mushroom and cream sauce. And to top it all off, a parfait aux fruits de la passion (passion fruit ice cream with grapefruit sorbet on top, all sitting in a pool of passion and strawberry coulis with orange sections and sliced strawberries for visual effects. Wow! This is my new resto préféré (favorite restaurant).

On the way home I stopped by my favorite place to wait — La Poste. The problem with this organization of postal fonctionnaires (bureaucrats) is that La Poste is not only for the mail, but it is also a bank where people go to deposit and withdraw francs. Quite frankly, from my experience, it is notoriously crowded unless you are in the middle of nowhere. I happened to be at the largest and busiest one, La Poste Centrale which stays open twenty-four hours a day.

After my expected wait, I headed to the Place de la Bastille and saw a huge contemporary art exhibit and met some of the artists. One, who's work I liked, paints nothing but clouds. How cool! Another was a photographer who takes only models for her work. One artist has two paintings on télécartes [the cards you buy in the tabac (cigarette shop) for use in payphones]. One kind thirty year old woman was an American who had become French by marriage. Artists are real.

Métro home for some huge long asparagus with soft boiled eggs for dipping and buttered toast. I especially enjoyed the strawberries with fromage blanc (a creamy white cheese almost like yogurt but ten times richer and better than our cream cheese) and sucre (sugar). Très correcte (Very proper)! Mom called and it was not only great to be on the same line with her but also to be on the same wavelength. She always inspires me to go for it. I'm going for it now. Bon voyage demain (Happy travels tomorrow)!

Paris, Nantes, vendredi 3 mai

Ever notice how many Parisians have their bookshelves in the room with the toilet [the bathrooms in France do not have a toilet, only a bain (bathtub) and/or a douche (shower), sometimes a bidet]? The WC or toilet in France is La toilette and the French are not embarrassed to say "where is the toilet?" Yes, there one finds works by many of the greats—Flaubert, Balzac, Hugo, Pagnol, Levy, Stendhal, and the list goes on. It's certainly more interesting than a plant I suppose.

In class we talked about a book called La Goutte d'Or (The Drop of Gold) and it turns out that the most dangerous rue in Paris is also called La Goutte d'Or. The story sort of goes like this: a Frenchman takes an Algerian's picture in Algeria

A Taste Tempting Sight In The City Of Light

and the Algerian thinks he has stolen his soul, so he travels to Marseille, a city with many Algerians, to try to find the perpetrator and the picture. C'est fou (It's crazy)!

What's not crazy is the fact that for the second day in a row, I had lunch at Au Bon Accueil — un verre de Côtes de Beaune et un verre de Côtes du Rhône (two glasses of red wine), seafood aspic with leeks and the traditional French moutarde vinaigrette salad dressing, seared rare tuna with incredible purée of potatoes and veggies. Then a sweet — crumble tiède aux pommes avec caramel (warm apple crumble with caramel sauce) and coffee. Now that is what I call Lunch!

Packed and psyched for my trip, I rode the bus to La Gare Montparnasse where I killed some time, drank a little nasty cold red wine, and called my brother A. All was well in Huntersville, but I had a TGV (Train à Grande Vitesse) to catch, so I said goodbye and retrieved my carte téléphonique. In Nantes, Cécile and her children couldn't find me nor I them, so luckily, I remembered how to get to her house. I took the tramway to the "Manufacture" stop, got off, and walked to la maison. Shortly thereafter, Cécile arrived, we caught up a bit, and she bathed and fed the children. My friend is a great painter and so creative, equally so in the kitchen. This day she prepared outstanding Sangria — sangria wine, oranges, kiwi, cinnamon, and Cointreau orange liqueur.

When her husband Laurent arrived we had another glass of the sweet and spicy concoction and headed for a Tapas Bar (not a Topless Bar) called La Bodegas and it was super fine. More sangria and a platter of everything — calamari, shrimp with heads, fried minnows which were my favorite, miniature octopus, potato omelette, Bayonne ham (raw), Serrano ham, dry sausage, hot chorizo beef stick, olives and bread. I love food orgies like that! Of course you end up drinking more than you eat, but, hey, were in France.

We drove by the twelfth century cathedral with its changing colored illuminations flashing against the outside stone of the church (sounds gaudy but it's really beautiful) and returned home for some dodo. Bonne nuit!

Nantes, samedi 4 mai

First thing this morning we took a trip to LeClerc, a grand grocery store full of all kinds of delicacies not found in its American counterparts. There is no doubt in my mind that the most sophisticated and demanding consumers and most educated gastronomically have to be the French. They simply have it all, and it's all delicious, even their canned and frozen foods are très bon avec beaucoup de gôut (very good with lots of flavor). Even the munchie "junk" food for eating with an apéro is delightfully tasty as well. La Vache Qui Rit (The Laughing Cow) cheese squares in the flavors of salmon, ham, blue cheese, and seafood are excellent before a meal, and so are the bacon flavored crispy bite size crêpes. I could go on and on. The instant tabouli in a can that the kids were eating even tasted quite good. The French wouldn't have it any other way. At a very early age children here begin to learn of the subtleties of taste by being given opportunities to try almost everything, cheeseburgers and chicken fingers excluded except for the occasional trip to the local McDo. Food is everything in France. C'est tout (That's all)!

For our excursion to Pont-Aven, a quaint village near Lorient, full of galeries of regional art, I prepared long buttered baguette sandwiches, piling on the ham, cheese, and lettuce. Although the weather was overcast, I took loads of photos anyway. Cécile's work here in Gallery B is beautiful. She has changed her style a bit, though she still uses bright colors in her evocative Van Goghesque scenes.

Down the rue at a simple café, I had hot chocolate, Cécile

drank hot milk, Laurent sipped a Gold (French beer), and the three kids downed a Coke with sugar cubes in it. Gee, and the French think Americans eat too many sweets!

Always in the region of Brittany, we made the two hour drive back to Nantes for what else? Another meal! The Sangria with Cointreau was flowing freely among the eleven of us there for a half-Italian half-French dinner which hit the spot that seems to be getting bigger—spaghetti Boulognese (meat and tomato sauce), salad with endives, delectable wonderfully stinky cheeses, four or five different red wines, sorbets, and coffee. Truly "under the influence"! Dormez bien tout le monde (Sleep well everybody)!

Cécile's Children Playing

Nantes, dimanche 5 mai

Today we arose and took le petit déj consisting of coffee and a specialty of the region, Kouign Aman (heavy flaky sugary buttery Elephant Ear-like pie). Laurent took me to the Nantes Cathedral so I could see the light photographically. It's such a beautiful edifice of the Lord! The inside is all lit up with light pouring through the large stained glass windows on high, a very challenging thing to capture on celluoid. On verra (We'll see)!

For lunch we had buttery omelettes and a spinach dish with even more beurre français (French butter) and little morsels of smoked bacon called lardons and cream. Wow! No wonder I like this dish so much. It's pure richness! And even more Kouign Aman for dessert.

Such a sunny day and so pleasant outside! Sophie-Marine, the babysitter who wants a five month job in the U.S., came by to say "Bonjour," and I broke it to her easy that jobs like that without a green card were next to impossible unless she worked as an au pair.

À la gare (To the station)! Everybody saw me off on the quai of the station, and now I'm journaling on my way to Paris. I couldn't help but think that I almost made it through a weekend with French people without someone asking me what I do or what I'm going to do, but just as I was climbing into the train Cécile asked me what I would do with my summer. I just said, "La même chose" (The same thing) and was gone. How could I be any clearer? You see, in France it is considered impoli (rude) to ask someone you have just met what they do for a living. If you know them well ça va de soit (that goes without saying). Par contre (on the other hand) in the States it is often

A Glimmer of Light in the Cathedral of *Nantes*

the very first question asked. Now, I know that my friend was only curious, because quite frankly, my friends here see me as a guest, not as someone working on a project. France is my work, she is my pleasure and my maîtresse (mistress). My friends in France really don't know what I do back home. I tell them I'm a photographe, but they never hear me. Between us, let's just say I'm gainfully self-employed in an endeavor of the soul, following my heart. C'est ça (That's it)!

Cécile wants two of my cibachromes (large high quality prints from slides), the one of the light green angel bust in white light and the cover of my last book, the bell tower of Saint-Tropez. Evelyne wants the boats in blue from Port Louis. And when I see my other friends they will get a chance to choose a "graph" for their walls. Just my token of appreciation!

Once in the City of Enlightenment, without thinking, I instinctively got on bus #92 and rode to L'Ecole Militaire where I stepped off, turned around and found just what I wanted—a cab. I love this syncronicity! At home I organized my things, got my camera, and took off for La Tour Eiffel to meet Sheila for dinner at Altitude 95 (one of two restaurants high above the city, this one being 95 meters up the tower). Great view! I had a salad with soft-boiled eggs, chicken breast in a cream sauce, and haricots verts ("air e co vair") (green beans). The Bordeaux was not memorable as we left half the bottle.

France for me, depuis qu'elle est ma maîtresse (since she has been my mistress) is a fine lady of exquisite taste who always pleases her lover in the end. She may get restless, jealous, even uppity from time to time, but in the art of pleasure she will always gratify her lover and only him. Vive la France!

Paris, lundi 6 mai

I totally forgot to set my travel réveil matin (alarm clock), so my natural inner time machine did not know to wake me, alors , it was eight, but I thought it was seven until I heard the kids in the hall. Discombobulated, mais près pour tout (but ready for anything)! Same parisian morning ritual—métro, crèmes at the Hoche, only, late for class.

Today we talked about not only the worldwide stereotype of southerners but the sometimes accurate assessment of all peoples who live in what is considered to be the South. For example, my own stock, North Carolinians, and Sicilians, Bavarians, les gens du midi (French southerners), peoples of the region of Kazakhstan in Russia, and any southern part of almost every country on the planet, are stereotyped. From a survey taken in class, we all were in agreement that southerners worldwide were thought to be different from their northern counterparts in the following ways: Polychronic— less often on time for various and sundry rendez-vous (meetings), more laid back and relaxed, less intelligent, behind the times technologically, possessing cruder manners, less hard working, speaking with a funny accent, serving as the brunt of northerner's jokes, more preoccupied with l'amour (love and sex), smoking cigarettes and/or chewing tobacco and pinching snuff, hunting game with shotguns, driving wildly, especially during inclement weather from the North, having more soul and this list surely goes on. But, and this is a big Butt. The truth is, we are all a product of all our life experiences, and so no matter where you come from, you can escape the stereotypes, and believe me, there are just as many about the northerners

Notre-Dame

in this world. Fortunately, most of this jiving between the North and the South is in fun. Another stimulating class!

Must have been a little homesick 'cause I went back to Planet Hollywood for another Club sandwich and the American champagne—Coca-Cola. For the rest of l'après-midi (the afternoon) I wandered the streets, avenues, and boulevards of the city trying to frame that picture that speaks of universal aesthetics and appeals to many. No easy task! To me, the perfect photo, if there is such a thing, would have, color, depth of field, balance of tone in all four quadrants, a perfect horizon, and lastly and most importantly, individual style. Remember, this is the perfect picture in my mind that I aspire to achieve, not present reality. Should I ever reach this goal of perfection, I will have to retire. Speaking of retired, my feet were tired, so I paused for tea at the Hôtel Lutétia, another gorgeous five star in the City of Light.

Dinner was simple and that suited me just fine — radishes, sunny side up eggs, hash browns, and fraises (strawberries) with fromage blanc and sugar. Organized my affairs, read a card from the mystery woman, and wrote this. Salut!

Paris, mardi 7 mai

Picked up a "Paris Match" to read while sipping my two café au laits at where else— Le Hoche. Conversation class was about La Vache Folle (The Mad Cow Disease), and many of us believe that it's coming or has already arrived in France. C'est pas possible (It's not possible)! Life's too short to worry about things like that. I mean, are you going to quit eating beef for the rest of your life and become a pseudo-vegetarian? Not me!

Despite my lack of fear of the crazy cow lurking at Vesuvio Pizza, I ordered une tranche de saumon grillé (a slice of grilled salmon) and gnochi al gorganzola. Très bon et pas cher (Very good and not expensive)! Although I love red meat, I usually keep my consumption down to once or twice a week. The media in the United States has caused me to feel that this will be beneficial to my health and longevity; however, I'm of the belief that heredity and luck play a huge part. In fact, eating in moderation that which pleases you without feeling guilty is my personal recommendation point à la ligne (period).

After lunch I caught the #42 home where I mailed my box at La Poste located on rue de Lourmel in the fifteenth arrondissement. The wait was unusually short, and in no time I was on the #42 again heading in the opposite direction to the rond point des Champs Elysées, not to be confused with the world's largest roundabout— Place de l'Etoile around the Arc de Triomphe. I was early for my interview, so I stopped in fashionable Marithé François Girbeau for a quick look. Their T-shirts, of all things, appeal to me the most because they are very high quality and have several buttons at the collar.

Lina's is a high traffic sandwicherie on the prestigious rue du Faubourg Saint-Honoré that is also a gallery of art. Madame Carole had not arrived, so an attractive black girl offered me a quality café as if I needed to be more hyped up. Madame and her partner François arrived, looked at my portfolio and especially liked the photos of Paris. It was decided! In September I would have a show called "Paris and Her Colors." Pleased as Parisian pumpkin pie, I set out to find a good frame shop that didn't charge three arms and as many legs. The first gallery owner I found kindly directed me to a shop on the other side of town near Montparnasse. My curiosity led me to this nice man's neighbor who quoted me a price of between $200 and $250 per picture.

Maquereaux— Paris Fish Market

Quelle blague (What a joke)! In the States I pay around $70 a frame with single matting.

To celebrate my first show in France, I walked to Ladurée for some Ceylan au lait. What an excellent thing to do! Some time later, it began to drizzle as I was strolling along l'avenue des Capucines to L'Opéra where I ducked into a bar for a Carlsberg before continuing on to my friends' place. Guy and Catherine were in fine form when I arrived and we toasted with glasses of muscat d'Alsace, a somewhat dry white, German in style. We chatted for a while before walking along the rue des petits champs to an authentically old and quaint resto called Chez Georges. Even the waitresses seemed to have been transported in time from a bygone era. For entrées (appetizers) Catherine and I shared a salad frisée et oeuf poche aux lardons while Guy had a large bowl of all you can eat Harengs and potatoes in oil. My turbot grillé with rich creamy béarnaise sauce was delectable. Dessert, however, was disappointing—Charlotte aux poires avec coulis de framboises (Pear mousse surrounded by ladyfingers with purée of raspberries). Three décafs for three tired people and the métro Palais Royal chez moi (where I live).

Paris, mercredi 8 mai

Today was the End of La Seconde Guerre Mondiale (WWII) Holiday! Most of the magasins (shops) were open, so I bought some dress shoes and some books on French subjects at Brentano's, an excellent bookstore on avenue de l'Opéra which sells material in both French and English. Not too far away one finds the old and majestic department store called Samaritaine, and it was there on the other side of a métro sign (for color and effect) that I thought I took my picture of the day. Then I went to Au Bon Marché, the famous department store/food emporium near Sevres-Babylone Métro Stop and the Hôtel Lutétia, to work up an appetite for lunch. The Epicerie (grocery) is chock full of what we Americans call "gourmet" food while it is just usual groceries for the locals. Several tours around this department had me ready for more than mere sustenance, so after a detour, I set out to make a new culinary discovery.

My friend François Olivier and I took a coffee at Le Temps Des Cerises near La Bastille where the French people were liberated in 1830. François is an excellent photographer and he took my photo while I was sipping a glass of red wine— oops, I mean coffee! Then it was a métro ride across town back to Sevres Babylone.

This time I had to speak Italian because my incredibly nice waiter was from Rome. He really appreciated my efforts to speak his lingo, and you could tell that he may have had a little mal du pays (homesickness). Living in Paris, even for European foreigners can be difficult, because it is next to impossible to break into the Parisians' click-like

Author at *Le Temps Des Cerises*

world. Most likely, a man like this will have other Italian friends and maybe friends from other nations, but rarely French. Why? It's bizarre, but the French and especially Parisians are notoriously difficult to befriend. This goes back hundreds of years and could possibly be explained in the annals of a glorious past whose present has turned into banality in comparison. Is there some imaginary image that needs protecting, or is it just a case of cultural bashfulness? The endless perplexing debate goes on.

The Antipasti were super delicious—grilled peppers in Italy's life blood (olive oil), all kinds of 'shrooms, olives, little octopus called poulpe, large octopus parts, mussels, artichokes and tons more olive oil. Next I enjoyed their version of Bruchetta, toasted Italian loaf soaked in more olive oil with tomatoes, fresh garlic, and mozzarella. After a coffee, the gracious and most friendly waiter shook my hand and bid me "Ciao! A la prossima volta!" (See you later! Until next time)!

I made my trek over to the Rive Droite and licked a few store windows (faire léche vitrine) along the way until I stopped for afternoon tea and a chocolate crêpe with vanilla ice cream at L'Hôtel du Louvre. Now why do I feel sick? "J'ai mal au coeur."

Skipped dinner; however, I did make my rendez-vous with Jeanne-Marie who met me at the most obnoxious Irish bar called The James Joyce for drinks. The Paris Saint-Germain football (soccer) match was on the télé, so having a drink there was out of the question. We ended up having beers at the gratte-en-ciel (skyscraper) Concorde Hotel café and caught up a bit. As expected, Jeanne-Marie asked me all the usual questions. What would I do when I returned to the States? How would I make a living? When would I be coming back to Paris? At least one sensible question! Anyway, I've learned to ignore those most personal "none of your business but you can't say that" questions. Hey, the French love controversy. Do they now not adore the Eiffel Tower and the pyramid of the Louvre?

As evidenced by the honking and all the youth of Paris going nuts in the streets, the local Paris Saint-Germain a gagné (won) in Belgium. Walked back to the métro Porte Maillot and rode home without incident. Didn't expect one. The French are so much more civilized after victories or losses than the English, Scottish, and Irish. Those nationalities' fans literally go bonkers after matches, and incidents abound.

Statue of *Henri IV* near *Place Dauphine*

Paris, jeudi 9 mai

Just for the record of generalizations, France is a country that is at once hyper-organized and yet in small ways confused all at the same time. Essentially monochronic (on time) and orderly, the French herd like cattle instead of forming a queue, so breaking in "line" here is rampant. If there is a line, néanmoins, the French will get in it and wait regardless of what for. French people refuse to wear the hood of an impérméable (raincoat) no matter how hard it's raining. Only tourists do this. In such a city as Paris, no one ever seems prepared for a downpour. Soaking wet heads will walk before they ever stoop to a light sprint to reach their destinations. You can always spot a tourist running.

During Spring and Fall if the temperature is between sixty and seventy degrees you will see people wearing heavy winter-type clothing even in the warm métro. In museums, instead of a leisurely viewing, they study paintings and other works of art as if they had to go home and reproduce the very work itself. No two bureaux de change will offer you the same exchange rate for the same amount of money. You are more likely to be struck by the mirror of a moto (motorcycle) while standing on a curb than by a city bus. Night clubs don't get started before midnight (maybe to keep the sorefooted wornout tourists in their hotel beds instead of on their pistes de dance (dance floors), so those who partake party til the wee hours, have their soupe à l'oignon (onion soup) at one of the few restos that still serve dinner at six heures du matin (six AM), go home, seul ou avec partenaire (alone or with a partner), and sleep away half a day, only to feel like merde for the duration of the afternoon. And music here costs twice as much as it does in the States, something about a TVA (Tax Value Added) of up to 33 percent for luxury goods. C'est affreux (It's ridiculous)! Note: I'm not claiming that all of these peculiarities of life are unique to Paris. It's just that they are so obvious to a frequent visitor here.

If there is a Heaven on Earth it can probably be found at a dinner table in France. We all have to eat. Some of us can choose what we eat. In France, it is an art to eat. Here, eating is supposed to be Heavenly. All the French know this. Food is so expensive, because it is so highly valued here. Americans value professional basketball players. That is why we pay them so many millions of dollars and then on the way home from the big game we treat ourselves to a Big Mac and a Coke. Our emphasis is more on convenience than on quality. Speaking of which, I had an enjoyable lunch on the Ile Saint-Louis today at the old Le Tastevin where I tried the rabbit terrine and the strangest French concoction—honey and lemon chicken. The terrine was out of this world, the chicken was bizzare but edible, and the apple strudel bathing in a rich sabayon sauce pleased the palate nicely. By the way, I'm getting rather attached to having wine with my lunch. It sort of softens what is already quite relaxing and enjoyable. The owner of the Tastevin offered me a glass of Cabernet Franc which completed the meal. I also witnessed a ninety-year-old lady eat a full three course meal, profiteroles and all. If I live to be ninety, I hope I will enjoy eating that much, too.

Later, near La Place Dauphine, I shot the beautiful horse and rider, a magnificent statue of Henri Quatre. It stands on the Left Bank side of the Pont Neuf where one can catch the Vedettes (boats) de Pont Neuf for a Seine River tour.

At this moment, I am having tea, writing this entry, posting the article and picture of me (Remember Evelyne in Vichy?) to my Mother, and writing a postcard to the mystery woman. Home to dine on baked endives, potatoes, some kind of meat, and asparagus. Early to bed—no disco tonight!

Paris, Nice, vendredi 10 mai

Well it's a miracle! Someone had hung my "lost" coat on the rack inside the corner café. How civilized can you get? Needless to say, I felt lucky again. I celebrated with two crèmes, and five postcards later, here I am again writing to the mystery woman. "We are two mysteries in the night orbiting one another with written words, discovering, yet unable to pierce the veil of long distance communication, both hungering to know more, searching for that lost equation, a never to be quenched desire that tugs our hearts and wearies our souls, and yet, gives us the hope and the will to go forward in a world that cannot recognize what we seek." How's that for a postcard?

After packing, I joined Madame for an impromptu picnic I put together in town—red wine, Bayonne ham, various hard goat's cheeses, brebis sheep cheese from the mountains, and a banette (like a baguette with pointed ends and made from a special kind of flour). We chatted about relationships, what is love, et cétéra and I caught a cab to Charles DeGaulle airport. Note: Boarding for this domestic flight was ultra early and twenty-five minutes before departure we were transported to the Airbus A320 appareil (plane) in navettes (shuttles). Glad I was early! In no time we were climbing through the clouds high above the gray to the sunshine and a glass of champagne. Yes! I love to fly! Beats walking! Such a feeling of total loss of controlling tendencies! You're just suspended miles up in an aluminum tube, at the mercy of well-trained pilots (you hope), and destiny. But you have given up your ability to control your own fate, and that is why I sit back and let le destin take me where it will.

Reflections At The Port Of *Vieux Nice*

Nice was nice and warm and partly cloudy. In my rental car I sped through town, stopping several times in no parking areas to take pictures on the spot. What a colorful town on the cool mint blue Med! At Le Vieux Port I photographed the colorful boats and the reflections of the nice pink and mauve buildings and the orange and yellow ones, too. I shot a freshly painted building in the old section of town that caught my eye for color and texture. Seems to me, southern towns paint their buildings more colorfully than northern ones, and in the States our houses are often dull grey, white, or no color at all. Monaco was there, along with the famous Casino, but Menton was my destination. I got an inexpensive room overlooking the sea at the Hôtel Prince De Galles right where the city limits begin.

Just down the road I had an enjoyable meal at the Solenzara Pizzeria—half a Spanish melon filled with porto, a pizza au feu de bois (pizza cooked in a wood fire oven) with mushrooms, ham, cheese, and tomatoes. Oh yeah! Lots of that hot and spicy peppery olive oil that is the crowning touch for any good pizza. The cheap vin de table (table wine) was also a delight. I spoke to all of my neighbors sitting nearby from Bruxelles, Annecy, and the Côte d'Ivoire (Ivory Coast) of all places. Bonne nuit!

Spices In The *Cour Saleya*

La Côte d'Azur, samedi 11 mai

Comme d'habitude (As always), when I stay in French three-star accommodations, I took my petit déj in the room and then set out to explore the village of Menton with my eyes and lens. Up and down steep hills without steps, I discovered that this mediterranean bastion of tranquility overlooks the sea best from the perspective of the old church which did have steps. On my way to lunch, I ran into a young couple who had their little dog in a basket on the handlebars of a bicyclette (bicycle). At the touristy Riviera restaurant I had tagliatelli with smoked salmon in a coral cream sauce with tomatoes, lemon and parsley. With a Coke to wash it down, I was impressed by the quality of my meal. C'était bon (It was good)!

The major roads along the Blue Coast are the Basse Corniche which winds around closest to the sea and scenic villages, the Moyenne Corniche which runs higher up in the hills lending a bellevue (beautiful view), and the Haute Corniche which is the express way to travel high above the blue and through tunnels, yet missing most of the beautiful scenery.

After buying some film, I drove the Moyenne and the Basse Corniches back to Nice where it took me approximately one hour before I finally found a small parking space. When I stumbled upon the market of the Cour Saleya I found some very colorful spices to shoot among other mouth-watering delights. Afterwards I drove outside the city and took more pictures of whatever looked interesting. Further ahead I stopped at Saint Jean Cap Ferrat, but there was really nothing to shoot because of all the walls surrounding the fine homes. Imagine that! Such an expensive piece of Real Estate! As with humans, the beauty there is within those walls we build.

At dinner I met two New Zealanders who were very friendly, and although they sat at another table, we spoke during the entire meal. Le Petit Prince is a fine restaurant which served me a salad with cured raw ham, du bon vin de Bandol (some good Bandol red wine), à point (roasted to pink perfection), sliced duck breast with all kinds of veggies and gratin de courgettes (zucchini) et tomates. Que c'était bon (My how it was good)! Naturally, we talked about why we were there. I was pleased that my new found friends were hip and very positive about what I do. Those people are insightful and bien élevés (well raised)!

Olives At The *Nice* Market

Menton, Saint-Tropez, dimanche 12 mai

Don and Colin woke me for breakfast, and after I was packed and ready to go, we met downstairs to exchange business cards and drink coffee. After returning to the open market of Nice to shoot the grand assortment of olives that only France can boast, I took the shoreline route to Saint-Raphael where I enjoyed a meal of fresh fried squid over spaghetti noodles with that spicy mayo sauce (rouille) they use to accompany soupe de poisson (fish soup).

Instead of going directly to Saint-Tropez I detoured over to the beautiful little village of Grimaud in the hills which offered me many photo opportunities in a very short period of time. I felt like I was the only person there on that Sunday afternoon. When I arrived at the Deï Marres I was welcomed and shown to #7, my personal room in which I relaxed while a Spring thunder shower came upon this beautiful southern land in the south of Paradise. With the windows wide open and the rain pouring down, I lay on my bed and thanked my lucky stars that I was in France fulfilling an ancient dream. Since I've been in the country this trip, that's the first downpour we've had. Quelle chance (What luck)!

Everywhere in the air is the scent of a wonderful flowering bush, an unidentified one with tiny yellow flowers. Simple things like that and the thunder and rain are comforts when you are far from home alone. There is a kind of familiarity in it all. Speaking of which, my friend Robert and his biking partner arrived totally drenched to the bone. We all headed for the bar for some warm rosé on ice and some catching up. No one had changed in the short year I was gone.

When I got hungry (the French would say "angry" because h is always silent), I rode in to town for dinner at Café des Arts and had eggplant provençale, pâtes au pistou (pasta with pesto sauce), and a bottle of the local vin de pays (inexpensive wine of the country). After dinner I called Michelle and Alain in Saint-Mâlo, Philippe in Lorient, Janine and Alain in Perpignan who have invited me to visit soon, and my Dad in the USA. I couldn't help but think about last year's joy and utter bliss being with my friend Constance in that very same corner of Avallon. But she set out for the footlights, and I took off to find the sky.

Saint-Tropez, Cassis, lundi 13 mai

Breakfast in bed on this cloudy matin (morn) that evolved into a sunny day as I drove to Bandol where I walked around and took pictures of the fishing net repairers among other things. These guys are quite talented with fixing the holes that develop after long days of fishing. On the way, however, I stopped the car at a little church in the middle of nowhere and discovered that my camera had been jarred and the dial that says +2+1 0 -1-2 was set on +2, so all of my photos taken on that setting will be overexposed two stops. Merde! The question is how long had the camera been on that setting. Almost all of my pix could be lost. A prayer was in order. If it weren't for the little church I might have never made this all important discovery. What was certain was that my exposures would be normal from then on.

Anyway, I checked in at the Royal Cottage Hotel and walked down to the old port to lunch on a salade niçoise. Most of the afternoon I took pix of the buildings and boats and whatever looked interesting. On the way home I picked up some things at the grocery store. Late in the day, I washed my dirty clothes in the bidet (I knew there was a use for those things) and hung them on the porch. With a change of clothes, I was headed back to the activity of the port where the sun was now illuminating different aspects of the small town. I met a photographer named Gregorie who told me when and how to see the famous calanques (the deep, narrow, creeks of the Mediterranean sea)—"go to the port, ask for Michel in the red boat, and take the very last excursion of the day to capture the best light!"

What happened next was classic. I took a fascination to the locals drinking various degrees of that golden réglisse (anisette-like) beverage called pastis. One of them could have been Gerard Depardieu's older brother if he even has one. They joked and let me take their pictures and insisted that I sit down for one of the same on the rocks with water, in other words, a cloudy yellowish looking liquid. Even though I can think of only a few things I hate worse, I partook so I could get a feel for what it's like to be a local. We talked, they drank, and I shot. They joked and I drank. In fact, I had to pry myself away from them so I could, one, stop drinking that God awful licorice flavored stuff, and two, so I could continue to catch the last light of the day.

Bandol Fishing Net Repairer

They were pleased to have had me "on the verge" of conversion, and invited me back anytime.

Quand la nuit était descendu (When night had fallen), I enjoyed a real cocktail called a planteurs with fruit juices and rum before dining at La Vieille Auberge. For an appetizer I had the specialty of the region— soupe de poisson (fish soup) complete with croutons, shredded cheese, and its rouille (spicy hot mayo). Although full after all that, I continued with escallope de merlan au basilic which was a lightly battered and sautéed filet of fish sitting in a tomato provençal sauce with basil. Since it was a "Menu" I was obliged to have dessert called pomme chaud et froid (whole baked apple, cored, in a caramel and raspberry sauce with the "froid"— a scoop of vanilla ice cream on top). Très bon and très full!

Door In Port Of Old *Cassis*

Cassis, mardi 14 mai

This entry is dedicated to the memory of my friend Roger Lane and his new bride who were aboard the horrible Value Jet crash in Florida only days ago. My brother informed me of the tragedy when I just happened to call him to say hello. Roger was a good man.

After a few pix here and there, including a beautiful blue door in the old part of Cassis, I drove the 23 kilometers to the town of Marseille where I experienced a kind of perfection. First, I must say that I've never once set foot in this Mediterranean megacity, and yet not once did I get lost in France's third largest city. I saw everything I intended to see—Notre-Dame de la Garde, the other famous cathedral, the quaint fishing village called Vallon les Auffes, the port, and les plages (the beaches). Not the most user friendly city in France, Marseille is full of immigrants still struggling for an identity. I certainly wouldn't frequent just any part of town at night.

Once back at the Royal Cottage, I enjoyed taboulet and a salade verte and a Coke by the cold crystal clear pool. Nap time! Washed more clothes in the bidet and went to the port for a series of self indulgences after getting the bad news—a café then elsewhere pistachio ice cream, a beer, and then a glass of wine. I was torn up but had no one to relate to but the sea. I wrote postcards to at least express myself on paper to friends, and then I just wrote in my journal. After a hot shower, I drove directly to the Prêsqu'île (literally means "almost an island"—a peninsula) Restaurant and dined royally. They botched my filet mignon, so they prepared another and comped an exquisite smoked salmon salad to boot, framboise eau de vie (raspberry water of life brandy), and a mediocre Backgammon Cuban cigar. The Bandol wine, not to be confused with the rather sweet red Banyuls from the Perpignan region, was splendide as well.

Called Mom and our conversation was sad, except it is always good to hear her voice. Being alone, one is forced to entertain even the most excruciating thoughts without being able to express them to the outside world. I was sad, but the following thought came to mind: "Death is often a sad conclusion for those who are living and a new bright beginning for the departed." Adieu, mon ami!

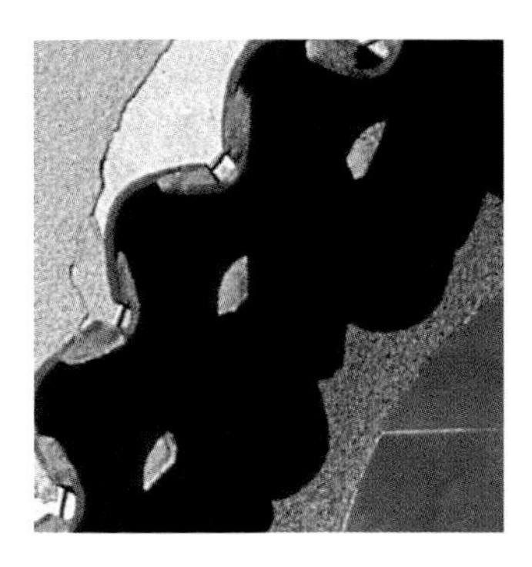

Cassis, Aix-en-Provence, Crillon-le-Brave, mercredi 15 mai

When I arrived in Aix, I took a huge risk by taking the first parking spot I could find, just on the outskirts of the CBD (central business district). As I walked around I suffered through the worry of having all of my worldly possessions volés (stolen). Mind games! But real! We've all heard the stories about getting ripped off in France. Not the kinds of thoughts you want to have while you are trying to create a potential masterpiece! I took pix of interesting scenes and I especially liked the dripping Bird Bath Fountain of Aix. Too bad, but I sort of hurried to soothe my conscience and wound up back at the car, windows intact. Yes!

On the route I stopped at Carpenteras for lunch at a simple local dive on the periphery of town. This hole-in-the-wall place served me pâté en croute (country pâté with a tasty crust), lapin roti avec des pâtes (roasted rabbit with pasta), fromage and mousse au chocolat. The rabbit came with des abats (entrails) and very little meat, but the pasta in that rich brown sauce was excellent.

Since I was two days ahead of schedule, I decided to try getting my room early at the now famous Hôstillerie du Crillon-le-Brave to no avail. They were regretful; however, they made calls across the sun-drenched land and found me a room at a Chambre D'Hôte, a sort of glorified B&B, family-style. As the crow flies it wasn't very far, but driving the winding roads of Provence took about a day. Just a joke! Really about an hour including my short stop at the village of Venasque. At the picturesque town of Roussillon I had to ask directions from a

Fountain Of *Aix*

man who actually knew where this place was. I followed his indications and found a sign that read, "Mamaison" (My House). I guess I was there.

Marine and Tito greeted me and showed me to my room which could really be called a smartly yet simply appointed suite. They are the happy unmarried couple who successfully run this new and undiscovered restored farmhouse that has a pool and a garden full of flowers and ripe vegetables. I photographed the cats, the garden, the pool, the flavorfully decorated kitchen, the house, Marine, Tito, and everything else I saw. The nooks and crannies of this world lend themselves best to the palette of the artist within.

On the very same day I visited the villages of Apt, Bonnieux, and Lacoste, then returned to offer my hôtesse (hostess) a glass of red wine. Note: When in Provence the most common form of amusement is to drive around the region and visit the nearby villages, some of which date back many years. Marine accepted the wine with pleasure. I shot her picture and got invited to dinner. La gentillesse française (French hospitality)! Tito returned and showed me the stereo and TV room. What a cool "Mas" (farmhouse— don't pronounce the "s")! I offered him a drink and he gladly accepted. We all got more acquainted, and Tito went to find another bottle of regional vino which we finished off in a hurry. Tito's spaghetti of onions, olives, tomatoes, and barley malt instead honey was quite good. Très bon! Excellent conversation about cooking and the possibility of my finding a chez moi (my home) nearby! Au lit (To bed)!

Roussillon, Menerbes, Oppède-le-Vieux, Lumières, Gordes, jeudi 16 mai

Provence is celebrated for many reasons, but I believe the soul of this blessed corner of the globe lies in its little villages perched above fertile valleys and etched into the hills of old evergreens and rich French dirt. Marine advised me which ones to see today as I finished my second cup of that precious black stuff around the small metal table outside on the fresh cut green pelouse. Gorgeous day by the way!

My first stop was the famed red dirt cliff town of Roussillon where I meandered about and shot some of the scenery. Then I checked out Ménerbes and Lumières before having lunch at Oppède-le-Vieux in the only restaurant there. Before I go any further I must say that I was able to capture a photo of the Madonna at the church of Lumières. *Quelle beauté!*

As expected, lunch was quite good, however touristy, and I started with a terrine de légumes (carrot and green bean pâté) that came with a creamy red pepper sauce. Then I had spinach ravioli covered in a basil cream sauce with cheese. Excellente! The short but steep hike to the ruins of the church helped to digest some of the copious meal. The view is nice from on high, but there was nothing more memorable than the food. What's new?

Next, I went to one of my favorite hill towns—Gordes. It is literally a village built from the bottom of a hill to the top and all around. With the blue sky and white puff ball clouds in the background and the old buildings illuminated by white light, I hope I got some good clichés (photos). After walking for what seemed like hours, I stopped

Madonna In *Lumières*

for a Coke without ice. Note: The French are less fond of ice in softdrinks, and even the drivethru at McDo will only serve small portions of that precious cold clear stuff.

From a bled (a podunk town in the middle of nowhere) I made use of one of France's highest technologies—France Télécom. My Dad was fine and he wished me the best for the rest of my journey. Then it was back to Mamaison for cocktail hour(s). The beverage of choice? Good ol' regional vin de table! I met Tito's parents who live nearby, and we all drank some of that carefully aged grape juice. My new friends reminded me that they would be glad to help me find a reasonable house nearby if I wanted to live there. One more possible link in the chain of a long lost rêve (dream)! Encore du vin (More wine)!

Again, I was invited to an impromptu dinner chez mes amis (at the home of my friends), and what a treat for someone who would have otherwise had to dine alone. We had salade de mâche (watercress salad with mushrooms), tarte aux courgettes (zucchini pie), and apple tart. C'était bon! Before retiring to bed, we watched the film "Lust For Life" which is about a man who so desperately wanted to serve God that he practically gave up his mind in order to paint the hidden beauty inside his soul that will forever please mankind. And he never sold a painting? How depressing! Bonne nuit!

Mamaison, Crillon-le-Brave, vendredi 17 mai

I enjoyed my Petit déjeuner outside in the cool morning air with the other guests and said au revoir to Marine and Tito. Very nice sweatshirt weather! Laid out for some color around the pool and then, speaking of color, as I entered the house I caught the neighborhood cat drinking water from a caldron. What a sight! Luckily I was prepared for the shot. I had my camera with me the whole time. After a shower, I got gas in Apt, packed, and headed for the Hôstillerie du Crillon- le-Brave stopping at Ile-sur-la-Sorgue for some pictures. When I arrived at le- Brave I disposed of my bags and had a light lunch of terrine de la compagne (country pâté) and a delicious salad of red peppers, frisée lettuce, cukes, tomatoes, and balsamic vinaigrette.

Some friends from Wilmington have a restored house in the badly flooded village of Vaison-la-Romaine, and they urged me to visit this very special town while in France, so I did. I parked along what seemed like a creek with a towering bridge overhead, but it turns out that this was the river that has and could potentially continue to inundate the entire lower half of this often rain-weary village. When I saw the line of the highest water level I sort of gulped to think that such a rivière could rise to that great a height without warning in only hours. Scary!

On the way back I detoured via Crestet which was no big deal and definitely not worth the shakedown drive up and down a one-lane road with traffic coming and going. Washed clothes in the tub, then myself. I dressed for

Cat In The Caldron At *Mamaison*

dinner, and dined—but first a Kir Royal out on the terrace overlooking the valley and Mount Ventoux with black olives, petite flaky cheese pastries, and leek pie. Then dinner—warm chèvre (goat's cheese) sandwiched in pan-fried zucchini medallions and garnished with frisée lettuce, Margret de canard avec des poires et une sauce caramelisée (roasted sliced duck breast with pears and a caramel sauce. Stupendous! (I'm turning into a duck, and I love it.) Lots of exotic cheeses followed, then dessert which was a combination of chocolate mousse, chocolate sorbet, and biscuit au chocolat. As if that wasn't enough, they brought me a plate of amuse-gueules sucrés (sweet after-dinner mouth teasers). That put me over the edge of a great day in Provence.

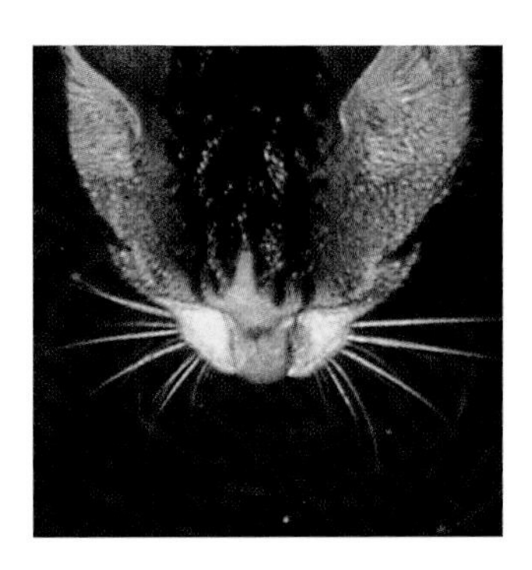

Crillon-le-Brave, samedi 18 mai

A nice couple from Hilton Head took their petit déjeuner in the salon with me this morning, and what a royal breakfast we ate on tastefully decorated trays—granola, yogurt, croissants, pain au chocolat, bread, butter, preserves, fresh fruit cup, coffee, and orange juice. If I had eaten but half of it, it would have almost been worth the sixteen dollars I paid. Note: Food in general is expensive in France, and breakfast is no exception. Fresh pâtisseries (pastries like croissants and brioche) are usually driven in daily from the nearest quality pâtisserie which coûte cher (costs a lot).

On this cloudy morn I visited several little towns or better yet wine villages like Gigondas, an excellent red, and Baume de Venise, a delicious sweet white. Inspired anew by the memory of the last time I was there, I drove to the town of Orange and syncronicity prevailed as the sun came out and I found a parking spot at the same time. The beautifully painted buildings caught my eye and much film was spent on them, but the ancient arène (arena) was temporarily closed due to an early evening concert.

Back at the Hôstillerie I had a salad and watched some tube. I find that although the French only have a few channels, their choice of programming is often very stimulating except for the many outdated and downright corny American feuilletons (serials). Later on, I was walking around town noticing the pleasant scent of anise in the warm Spring air, and it had to be natural, because there were no bars anywhere for kilometers. Note: Pastis, the licorice-flavored liqueur of preference, flows freely in France.

The Town Of *Orange*

Tonight there was a dinner to die for—celery mousse as an amuse-gueule, Baume de Venise muscat as the apèro with olives, asparagus wrapped in crustillant (thin crust pastry) in a garlic cream sauce and a bulbe d'ail confit (roasted garlic bulb), half bottle of Gigondas, grilled filets of Rouget (little white flesh fish with red skin), sautéed spinach, sliced pomme de terre (potatoes), and as if that wasn't enough, out came the sirloin with zucchini and goat's cheese, then more—an assortiment de chèvres (an assortment of goat cheese), and finally the perfect sweet nothing dessert which the French do so expertly that goes so well when you are already about to explode—strawberries and white chocolate mousse. Tres bon!

Crillon-le-Brave, Perpignan,
dimanche 19 mai

Breakfast in bed and then I paid un bras et une jambe for the two nights and several meals. However, I left very satisfied. Bonne route (Have a good drive)! I stoped at the N100 for a shot of a beautiful field of lavender and the Lubéron behind. There were cloudy threatening skies over Provence as I drove through Carpentras where I ate rabbit days ago, Avignon where the Pâpes (Popes) used to live, Nîmes where the great Roman Maison Carrée (considered by some to be the perfect monument) and Amphitheater proudly stand, Montpellier (I think I'm lost), then Narbonne, from where the great Henry of Narbonne hailed, and finally my destination, Perpignan where I somehow remembered how to get to Alain's and Janine's house. With open arms, they welcomed me into their home, and as usual, Janine was cooking something special in the kitchen while Alain straightened things up. We talked and drank a coffee together before I climbed to my room to unload my bags.

They had just made an addition to the house which Alain showed me. I would be sleeping in the office whose floor was now the ceiling for the dining room. In France, space is a very precious commodity, and none is wasted. Three other people were staying with my friends as locataires (boarders): an English school teacher, a guy from Iceland, and one from Norway. Overall, it was a Sunday lazy Sunday for me.

Around seven-thirty the parents of the boy from Iceland arrived, and we had apéritifs, nuts, and stuffed olives from neighboring Spain. When everyone was present, we began a

Lavender Field With The *Lubéron* Mountains In Background

marvelous meal of red wine from California. California? Oh yeah, over a year ago, I had sent my friends a bottle of Gundlach Bundshu Merlot, but they refused to drink it without me. Well, this night we were all together to enjoy what everybody agreed was an excellent wine. Note: There are many differences between California wines and French wines due to soil varieties, climates, methods, et cétera; however, similarities by the very nature of the grapes and the resulting wine must exist. The point is, different or similar doesn't mean better. Better is only a judgment the individual palate can make, and although there are wines selling for thousands of dollars here in France, such a wine would be wasted on my palate unless of course someone else was buying.

The surprise Catalonian dish was called "Poulet Gambas," a kind of surf and turf paella made from grilled chicken, shrimp with the heads and tails still on for flavor, yellow rice, vegetables, pine nuts, dry white sherry, olive oil, salt and pepper, and water with which to simmer the rice. Everyone was delighted with the delicious regional specialty, and for dessert we had flan-like custard and whipped cream rolled in genoise (sponge cake) and champagne.

It was great to be back chez les Perez in beautiful sun baked Catalonia (a region consisting of the northeast of Spain and the southern portion of France around Perpignan which has its own language, traditions, culture, and its own proud feeling of independence even though it is under the rule of French and Spanish governments), after being away for two years. I had stayed with this family before as a locataire when I was attending classes at the University of Perpignan. Bonne nuit, tout le monde (Good night everybody)!

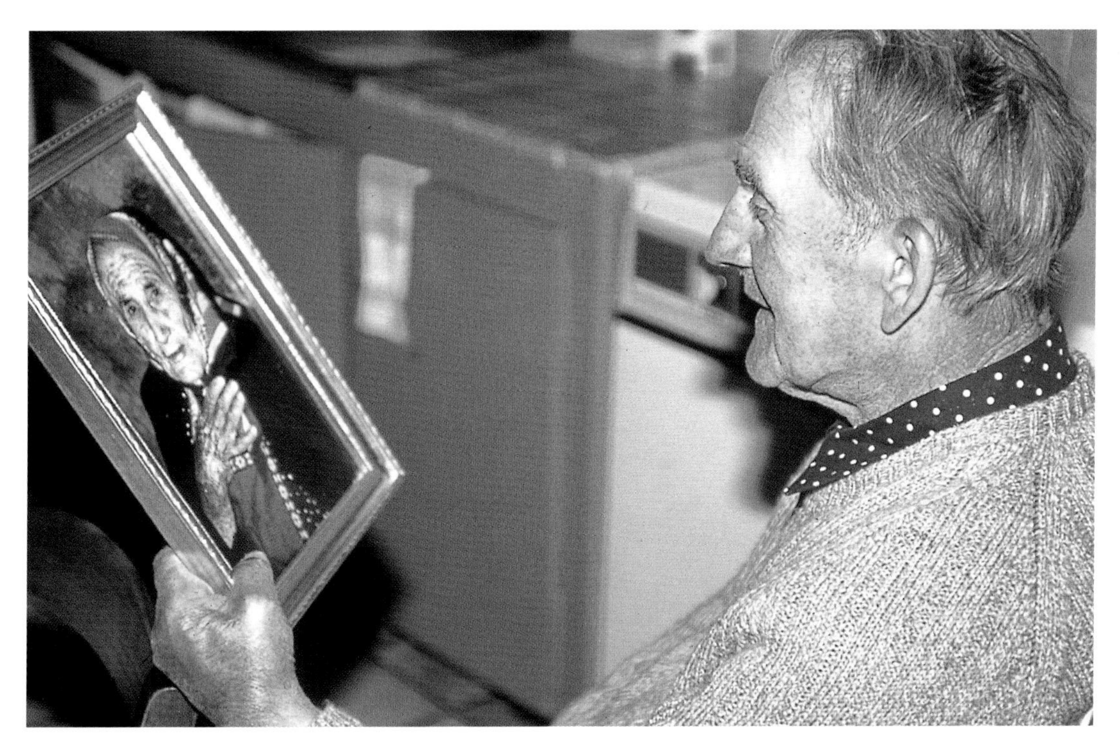

Picture Of A Picture In *Villefranche-De-Conflent*

Perpignan, lundi 20 mai

Got up and had coffee with Alain before driving to the centre commerciale (mall shopping center) called Auchan where I love to see all the wonderful edible things they sell. I bought some flowers for Janine, Williams mousse à raser (shaving cream), a magazine called "Le Nouvel Observateur", 1400 francs from a machine à sous (automatic teller), and un crème at the café.

When I returned, Alain and Janine were just sitting down to a typical French lunch, and they invited me to join them. We had Spanish Seranno ham, petits pains with butter, various cheeses, and red wine. It's next to impossible to skip a meal in France, especially if you are a house guest. Not that I want to skip a meal. Its just that sometimes I feel like eating is all I do here. Wonder why?

On my way to the village of Villefranche-de-Conflent I picked up two hitchhikers on their way back to Hotel School where they were learning about cooking and service (waiting tables). I drove them the extra five kilometers and doubled back to find Villefranche somewhat of a disappointment. The vieille dame (old woman) of ninety-three years was out of town, but I accidentally ran into her daughter, and she showed me the photo I sent them, all nice and framed. I felt proud. I took pictures of her and her paralyzed son with the photo in his hands. Very-heartwarming!

But this time something was definitely missing. Maybe part of it was because I had already discovered the place two years earlier, and then it could have been that this amazingly spirited grande dame (great woman) was absent, but still alive at least. That made me happy. I'll see her next year I'm sure.

It's nice to know that someone is watching over me. Today I was passing another car, and a motorcycle was coming head on towards me, and I had no choice but to play chicken with this imbécile. Although he had room to get over, he stayed in my lane until the second before impact at which time he leaned the bike over and missed me by inches. What a proud bastard! He almost lost his life for being such an egghead. I was seething mad, but not altogether surprised. European motorcyclists are flat out crazy to begin with, and incidents like that are probably quite common.

Happy to be alive and in one piece, I settled into a booth at the Auchan café for another grand crème. Back at the house, Janine was preparing yet another classic meal while Alain poured the apéritifs. Janine was happy with her orange fleur de lys. For dinner we had ham, endives, Spanish bread, the specialty of curried pork with lots of cream, butter, red peppers, and onions. Quite delicious! Then we had cheeses and chocolate pudding with whipped cream on top. Bons reves!

Perpignan, mardi 21 mai

Today I visited the beautiful seaside community of Collioure, just south of Perpignan, and walked around a bit. Things had changed. I was really disappointed that there were very few colorful boats on the shore and only one palm tree remained on the little boardwalk. I laid on the pebbly beach for an hour and a half until the sun had hidden itself behind the clouds. All the while, young men training to be marines were putting together and blowing up rafts on the beach for manoeuvres. An audience of young girls heckled them the whole time. Either they were anti-military or just plain cruel. I wondered if this was a French thing, Catalonian, Spanish, European, or just youth in general.

Crêperies are in fashion here, so I ducked in to one of the more popular ones for an excellent crêpe with ratatouille, emmenthal cheese and an egg. After a Coke sans glace (without ice), I took sealed boxes of fine cigars to La Poste and mailed them but forgot to put the most elemental thing on the label—U.S.A. Merde! Once again, like my film, I'll only know when I get home. Oh well! I've always been very lucky about things like that, so, no worries! On to the next thing—Cinq à Sec, a countrywide drycleaners with the familiar orange and black storefronts. Picked up some of my button-downs and got more cash with my weary Visa card. It works sometimes, others not. I often have to pay en especes or en liquide (in cash). I found some good ol' Jim Beam and some Bud (the name for Budweiser in Europe) in Auchan for a little taste of Americana for Alain.

In the town of Perpignan, I easily found a parking space and went into a jewelry store, finding just the specialty of the area I was looking for—a grenat stone cross in gold with a Catalonian Montage. It's a lot like Janine's. Hope Mom likes it! In the square, I met a beautiful young woman asking for donations for AIDS research. I gave her a hundred franc note, and she gave me a wonderful computer imaged photography book. She even let me take her picture.

When I returned home Alain and Janine were just coming in with the dog that had just gotten stitches from the thunderstorm the night before. Then Alain discovered what "Bill" sent him from America and was very pleased but qualified it with the fact that he didn't think "Bill" would get another presidential term. Alain had Jim Beam on the rocks and the rest of us had very cold Bud at 5 percent alcohol. Dinner was excellent as usual—tabouli with mint, green peppers, tomatoes, olive oil, et cétéra, baked whole salmon with lemon and crème fraiche, with baked tater tots which reminded me of home, and finally melon with bananas in muscat and of course, something to wash dessert down—more muscat. C'était bon!

I can't get over how knowledgeable Alain is. I could just sit and listen to his stories all night. He has worked all over the world, lived in China and Vietnam during the war, is half-Chinese half-French, remembers the English bringing them chocolate when he was fifteen, and is not real fond of America in the world of politics, but he likes me. C'est déjà pas mal (That's already not bad)! After Mandy (the English teacher) had gone to bed, we drank a little Icelandic Schnapps or "Black Death". Now I know where it got its name. À demain!

Beautiful *Perpignanoise*

Perpignan, Cadeques, Spain, mercredi 22 mai

Le printemps en France (Spring in France)! Up early for a petit déj with Alain and some grande magique (TV) until Mandy was ready to go swimming at Collioure and sightseeing in Spain. First we drove round and round the cliffs of the mountains ending at the sea, almost making my English friend car-sick. The roads were among the windingest I've ever driven, but finally we reached our destination, the little chalk-white fishing village of Cadeques. There, we split up so I could take pictures and she could bronze in the sun. There were all sorts of great things to photograph here because everything was painted white including the church, even the boats. Near the shore I found a Spanish painter who was conveying the light of this fine day on canvas. Overall, I would recommend this town to any photographer who is looking for something universal and beautiful in his frame. My favorite picture was the palmier or palm tree with the deep blue background and the white building behind it.

Mandy and I met up and decided on a little outdoor cantina for an "ensalada catalana" which consisted of charcuterie (salamis, sausages, ham, bologni, and other pork specialties) on lettuce, tomatoes, carrots, peppers, and olives. Très bon et très français (Very good and very French)! Pas cher (cheap), but we couldn't afford anything else without using a credit card at one of the full-service tourist restos.

Then poor Mandy tried to keep her mind off the edge of the cliffs as we wound around each turn for forty-five

Palm And White Buildings In *Cadeques*, Spain

minutes north to Collioure, never having to present our passports once during the petite excursion. The idea of a United Europe is slowly becoming a reality. Slowly! They have a very long way to go politically however. Anyway, in town we enjoyed a coffee in Le Café des Templiers where fishermen and artists alike have imbibed the precious black stuff if not some kind of alcoholic beverage to lighten the atmosphere. Later we walked around a bit and had a small private wine tasting in one of the shops. I bought some Muscat de Rivesaltes which is exquisitely sweet and fruity, making it perfect also for sweetening fruit salads.

Then came the excitement! While closing the trunk, the one and only key fell off the key chain into the trunk which locked shut. I immediately called Europcar Assistance in Paris. Not surprisingly, they told me it was not their problème because it wasn't a breakdown. Alors (Well), they put me in touch with the agency in Nice who didn't want to deal with me either. Finally, they told me how to get in the trunk from the backseat of this model car. When I hung up, Mandy was outside the cabine with THE key. A nice French couple had already showed her how to get into the trunk from the inside, and voilà la clef (Here is the key)!

I was still a little shaken, because you can imagine what a pain in the ass it would have been if we couldn't get in from the interior of the car. Oh well! When you don't have any major problems, then the little ones seem even bigger I guess.

I've been thinking a lot about how, if you believe in you, then you will believe in what you do, and if you believe in what you do, others will believe too. Bonne journée (Good day)!

Perpignan, jeudi 23 mai

Désormais (From now on) I'm translating my journal intime (diary) from French to English, so there'll be more foreign words to learn. And well, why? Parce que (because) I'm in France, learning the language all day long, alors (so), I am profiting from this opportunity to practice the art on the greatest canvas I could find n'est-ce pas (is it not so)? It's also a very good passe-temps (something to pass the time away).

After much searching and shooting in Collioure I found what I would call the most revealing shot of this little village on the shore. It includes another palmier, the small beach, the water that meets the shore, and the beautiful unmistakable orange tiled-roof church in the background.

A terrible thing happened to me and my precious diary in 1984 when my car and all of its contents were stolen in a suburb of Paris. My prize possession of all my belongings was in the coffre (trunk) at the time of the vol (theft), and except for my wonderful memories, almost a year of writing and pictures were lost forever. Today this loss has become my inspiration and driving force to share my most recent travel journals with you.

This morning when I was walking to town one of the neighbor's dogs bit me on the leg, but I decided to forget about it. There was some blood, but, hell, I didn't want to go to the local hôpital. Hopefully, this chien wasn't malade (sick). Recently the French politicians were to vote on whether to continue paying for the care of foreigners if they were injured in France. I think they decided to make non- citizens pay. C'est affreux (that's totally crazy)! With all the foreign travelers who visit France each year, spending loads of money, only very rarely involved in an accident, and the government won't pay the medical bill if the patient cannot. I hope my country doesn't have this same policy. Bon (hard to translate here, can mean "well" or "good", but here it's like "enough said")!

En ville (In town), I had lunch at The place to have lunch, a modern restaurant of glass and polished metal that specializes in dessert creations with or without their homemade glace (ice cream). I had a salade aux crabes (crab salad) which was actually a kind of purée of crab meat spread on Pôilane bread with a mixed salad on the side. On my way home I stopped for a grand crème outside of a café which was un peu dégueulasse (a little disgusting) because it was dirty and modern inside and located at the crossing of two busy roads and railroad tracks. Le bruit des moteurs, la fumé, et la poussière partout (the noise of the engines, the exhaust, and the dust everywhere)! It looked like an inspiration for a Francis Cabrel song.

Once at the house, I told Janine about the dog biting me, and she decided to help me locate its owners so we could find out if le chien was healthy or not. On n'a rien trouvé (We didn't find a thing), alors (so), Janine and I were d'accord (in agreement) to forget about the whole thing. Heinekens for everybody! Then with dinner we had kirs (white wine and sirop de cassis) for apéros, des Harengs à la crème et ognions (Herrings in an onion cream sauce) et de la terrine de canard à l'Armagnac (duck pâté with Armagnac). Alain prepared a side course which consisted of tomatoes, mushrooms, parsley, salt, pepper, and olive oil, while Janine made Lasagne out of the leftover salmon. For dessert we enjoyed sliced strawberries in their juices and muscat. Un bon repas (A good meal)! Ça va de soit (That goes without saying)!

Exotique Collioure

Perpignan, Nice, vendredi 24 mai

Janine and Alain fixed me a special breakfast for the long autoroute ride to Nice, and we said our goodbyes and à bientôts (see you soons) as I rolled away, dog bitten and all. Seems like I always have to wait for the future verdict of fate. Hey, I'm in France where I must think of good things and celebrate life! Around 13h00 I rolled into Nice and got a hotel room at an Ibis, a reasonably priced chain of highrise hotels with very spacesaving rooms and a full service restaurant downstairs. Oh, and free parking which is always a plus!

My next move was to walk the entire length of the famous Promenade des Anglais (Boardwalk of the English) which stretches between the oceanfront property and the hard pebble beach. I snapped a few pictures along the way as suntanned people strolled the sidewalk while others would come and go to enjoy the late afternoon rays of the Mediterranean sunshine. On my left was the most expensive Real Estate in all the land, and on my right was what belonged to everyone. Thank God for beaches! At the end of the Promenade I found the Vieux Nice (Old Nice) and an area full of attractive looking restaurants, each serving some kind of Spécialité Niçoise. What really caught my eye were the beautiful yellow and orange buildings in this place they call the Cour Saleya. To reward my inspiration, I sat outside one of the cafés with a crowd and enjoyed a grande Leffe (wonderful flavorful Belgian beer). Then I had dinner outside as well at a restaurant that cooked my Paella with white sausages, chorizo, chicken, pork, and what makes the rice all bright yellow— lots of exquisite saffron.

Pebble Beach Of *Nice*

Après dîner (After dinner), as I was walking through the Old Town I ran into two black Marines from America whose ship was anchored in the port of Villefranche-sur-Mer. One was from Wake Forest, North Carolina. Petit monde! This guy was très sympa (very nice), and he brought me up to date on everything going on in the NBA playoffs. I was quite pleased that Jordan and his Chicago Bulls were still winning, again! Then to show how popular and diverse this place can be, three "Christians" from Oral Roberts University who were there for a march and a rally, came along and prayed for all of us. A taxi took me back to the hotel and I called it a day.

Nice, samedi 25 mai

My natural alarm woke me just before the phone rang, and after a douche (shower) I descended for a breakfast of a cornucopia of things including cheeses and yogurt. Concentrating on where the action was, I returned to the Cour Saleya where there was an openair marché (market), one of the greatest places to get a feel for the French and their favorite commodity—la bonne bouffe (slang for good food). Needless to say, I shot my celluloid wad in hopes of capturing some special artistic effect, all the while conveying something truly French. The spice lady was quite nice to allow me to take her photograph, and she didn't even mind that I wasn't shopping for spices.

Today, even after seeing all that delicious food at the market, I skipped lunch to try to lessen what seemed to be becoming a heavier load. From now on, I'll try to eat well, but less. Right! I always go through this American-born angst when traveling through France. Just forget losing weight in this country, point à la ligne (period).

Speaking of food, I have a dream of opening a Traiteur (a glorified French delicatessen) where you can buy the following délices fabriqués à la maison (delights made on the premises): olives from everywhere, cheeses, Parma and Seranno hams, chorizo, chocolates, candies, all kinds of terrines and pâtés, les plats cuisiners (cooked dishes) like potatoes and whole onions, roasted peppers and garlic, roasted chicken, tapenade, hummus, tabouli, coffees, teas, pastries, breads, and lots lots more. There will be a self-serve type seating area where visitors can have lunch like the restaurant at Fauchon in Paris.

Spice Lady Of *Vieux Nice*

Each new day, there will be specialties to try and be enlightened by. You will always be what you eat. Garbage in, garbage out, right?

Buses here are easy to figure out, so I rode to Port de Nice on the #10 and stepped in to a café for a grand crème and some journal writing. People who are never alone in public are lucky in one respect, but I believe they also miss so much of the living that goes on around them and the quality thinking time. QTT is so vital for us all to gather our thoughts, sort things out, and just dream a little. People who are never alone miss out on daydreaming which I truly believe is good for health and happiness.

Two Leffes later in the Cour Saleya and I had that pleasant slight buzz before dinner. I picked Le Bistro Des Artistes and ate a mixed salad with morceaux d'anise (bits of anise) which actually tasted good with the greens. Next came what I had been craving all day—Pasta noodles with smoked salmon in a cream sauce. C'était si bon (It was so good)! You ask do I ever have a bad meal, and I say "yes" but rarely in France. Remember, chefs here of even average restaurants are more highly respected than their counterparts in the States, and they are often part owners of their establishments. Besides, its not like I'm eating in the cheapest places. My average meal with wine usually costs between 25 and 35 dollars with the tip included. Even just a Pizza with wine can cost that much. Note: In France, your gratuity is always included in the restaurant bill; however, some people like to add a little more to that amount. Speaking of adding, I subtracted some weight by walking the whole way back to the Hotel Ibis.

Nice, London, Sunday the 26th of May

Sweet dreams are made of these! Listen to this! D'abord (First) my travel agent in the U.S. misunderstood me when I asked for a coach class one way to London on Air France. But I was totally unaware of what she had done even when they told me to stand in the line which said "Plein Ciel". Thinking nothing of it, I tried to enter the Club to use the bathroom, but never presenting my ticket, they told me to go downstairs. C'était con (It was stupid)! Anyway, the blague (joke) was still on me thanks to Evelyne and my inattention to what was going on around me. Next, I got the seat assignment of 1F and it still didn't ring a bell, even sitting there up front, until the flight attendant began pouring The Real Thing to Frenchmen— champagne. Je suis con moi (I'm not too bright)! Accidentally, there I was in Première Class enjoying bubbly as I was being pressed against my seat rocketing for an English break of five jolly days in London Town. Note: I had to go to London to take the Eurostar Highspeed Train through the Chunnel (English Channel Tunnel) to the grand city of Art and Culture, so the following is a little of Britain from an American's Francophony perspective.

It finally sunk in after my third glass of Laurent Perrier, and I had come to my senses. Air France Flight 365 departing Nice with a destination of Londres First Class. Yes! It's good to be good to yourself! They brought out smoked salmon, rosbif à point (rare roast beef), a delicious kind of cole slaw made with celery root instead of cabbage, red wine, feuilleté de pomme (flaky apple pastry), fromage blanc with bread, and a café. Voila! I think the term "first class" had to come from France,

London Edifice Near Leichester Square

because they surely know what it means. Then came a novel experience as I rode in one of the old fashioned London cabs that have no creature comforts whatsoever and make a hell of a racket. My driver had little to say through the Plexiglas partition until he went up the wrong street for my hotel and had to look in his little book. No worries! In a jiff he had me at the Ruskin Hotel on the famous and somewhat quaint Bloomsbury Square. My room was spacious enough for one, and it looked out onto a sort of green area dividing it from the Haddon Hall Hotel.

Ah, good ol' English weather! Dreary! I went for a long walk without my "traveling companion" down to the river Thames (pronounced "Tims") where I followed the quai all the

way to Big Ben and the fabulous Westminster Abbey.
The drizzly climate seemed to greet me like an old friend, making buildings more severe and sort of enclosing me in a foggy late afternoon hue. Having heard that London is renowned for its great bookstores, I ducked into one nearby which also had a café inside. I took my tea with milk and sugar like the English do and rested my legs a bit. Later on I walked on up to the bustling Charing Cross district and checked out which entertainers were coming to town. Note: London may be the best city in the world for all sorts of concerts, performances, and theater. Check ticket offices in the city for dates and times. Often some of the best seats are still available for a price, even a day or two before the event.

My friend Dr. Unks, an Education professor at UNC who has been teaching groups of UNC-Chapel Hill students for summer sessions in Great Britain for over twenty years, is staying in the Haddon Hall with his group, and I wanted to call him. Well, the phone wouldn't seem to work. I tried and I tried but no dice, until for the second time today, I thought I was losing it. In order to use the phone you have to press a red button when it takes your money. I wasn't pressing the magic bouton. Again I felt like a con (dummy).

Bagging the phone, I decided to walk over and see what was up. There, I found a message from Dr. Unks telling me to meet him at The Plough, a popular watering hole for his students. I drank a warm ale called Fettey's which wasn't very tasty, but my friend never showed up. Hunger called, and I soon found an Italian restaurant where I had

Bruchetta, une salade "arucola" with pine nuts and Romano cheese, roasted potatoes with onions, and a demi-litre (half liter) of red wine. On my way back to the room I stopped by the pub again and voilà Dr. Unks! We caught each other up to date, closed the place and went back to our hotels. Note: London pubs are required by law to close around eleven every night. If you want later excitement you can go to one of the many clubs which stay open until the wee hours. Good long day! Cheerio!

London, Monday the 27th of May

Today was Pentecôte, a religious holiday that they call a Bank Holiday en Angleterre (in England). Many shops and businesses were closed, the weather was still dreary, so I enjoyed a typical copious English breakfast in the basement of this fine establishment. Unlike their French neighbors, the British usually have things like brown toast, eggs of all sorts, smoked bacon, sausage, cornflakes, and of all things baked beans, and sliced tomatoes. Yes, they have coffee and orange juice, and this remains one of, if not the biggest meal of the day here.

At 9h30 I had a rendez-vous with le docteur (my friend) and I brought my camera in a plastic sack for protection against the English rain. The first thing we did was take the "underground" (subway, or tube) to Tower Hill where one finds the Tower of London and the Tower Bridge, both popular tourist attractions which we passed up this time. Instead, we took a touristic boatride up the Thames to Westminster where I was hier (yesterday). I P-graphed the bridges and buildings despite the mauvais temps (bad weather), and even though this excursion was semi- guided I didn't understand un mot (a word). Must be the language barrier! Since it was almost twelve, we decided to wait for Big Ben to sound, but the traffic on the wet roads really drowned out the wonderful and strangely familiar bells. Tant pis (Too bad)!

Our next move was to find a pub for a self-service kind of lunch. Pubs are notorious for having cheap eats called "pub grub" which vary from correcte (acceptable) to not-so-hot. Pubs often have elaborate welcoming signs outside their entrances, and I thought this one made a good rainy weather subject.

Fuller's Pub In London

Note: The English have a different attitude towards food than the French, and thus, their cuisine has never really developed into what one would call fine. In fact, it is commonly known that the Brits cannot faire la cuisine (cook). Sure, there are some French-trained English chefs who can dazzle in the finer hotels; however, the list of dishes that are truly English is a short one and probably needs salt and pepper. I had the vegetarian plate of slaw, celery salad with nuts, mixed salad, and bland vegetable lasagna. Dr. Unks showed me that a "scotch egg" was a hard boiled egg wrapped in breading and deep fried. Novel, I thought, but not too terribly tasty. Hey, I can be a food snob with the best of them. I admit it.

We took a quick ride in the tube to Charing Cross where I bought two tickets to the Neil Diamond concert tonight at eight. Only in London can you get tickets to a "to be sold out" event on the very day of the show! Back to the hotel for my siesta. I appropriately listened to Elton John's "Made in England" and napped for a while until tea time. Note: I heard that High Tea was something for tourists only, that the locals never partake in such a thing. All I know is, afternoon tea or coffee is almost as civilized and rejuvenating as a short afternoon nap.

At five thirty Dr. Unks and I met to go to Baker Street to take the train to Wimbly Arena and to find a nearby restaurant before the show. A nice black man directed us to a Greek restaurant up the way where we dined quite well—Beaujolais wine, Greek hors d'oeuvres which were delicious, salad, moussaka with a lot of red meat (I decided not to worry about the Mad Cow tonight), and apple tart. The concert was beginning when we arrived, and very polite custodians led us to our fifth-row seats near the rotating circular stage.

Neil Diamond was super! He played all of his greatest songs plus a few new ones like the excellent piece his son wrote. Man, he sang "Sweet Caroline," "Cherry Baby," "Holy Holy," "Traveling Salvation Show," "Coming to America," and many others. It was stupendous, and the énergie and enthusiasme were contagious. Even Dr. Unks, who had only heard of Neil, really enjoyed himself. Quel spectacle (What a show)!

London, Tuesday the 28th of May

"Où est le soleil?" are lyrics from one of Paul McCartney's lesser known songs; however, it is plain to see when you are in his country where he got his inspiration. I said the very same thing today, "Where is the sun?" Bloody bad weather again!

Just before leaving the hotel I ran across a basket of milk bottles which reminded me of when I was a child and milk was delivered daily to my house in clear glass bottles. Now that was civilized if you ask me, but it's just not done anymore where I'm from. The shot of these milk bottle tops seemed to make an artistic photo of things which repeat, just my style.

What do you do during rainy weather in London? You either go to a museum, see a matinée performance of theater, walk around in the rain, or go to Herrod's on Knightsbridge which is a London institution. It happens to be the finest department store in England, selling everything from Haute Couture to gourmet food in the "Food Halls." I was inspired to take note of some of the wonderfully prepared dishes like Taramasalata (a Greek creamy pink fish egg spread), Tzatziti (cucumber and mint sauce), Hummus (purée of chick peas, garlic, and olive oil) veggie kabobs, grilled vegetables, miniature vegetables—probably from France, tomato/mozzarella, basil, carrot, cauliflower, and leek terrine in gelatin, three-pepper terrine in gelatin, little onions à la grecque, cornichons, and topped and tailed green beans. Note: This is no Fauchon; however, it is just as expensive and they deliver to your home.

I walked up K-bridge, ate a slice of pizza on the street and continued to Leicester Square where I shot despite the temps (weather) and went back to the Ruskin to relax. Note: When you only have a few days to see all the museums and monuments of a monstrous city there is rarely time to relax or nap in your hotel room, but you can always duck into a coffee shop and recharge your batteries. If your hotel is centrally located, then changing for dinner is much more convenient than going to the restaurant looking like a wet tourist in tennis shoes.

Around six, I met Dr. Unks and all of the UNC students. The entire group of us rode to the National Theater Complex in an old fashioned Double-Decker Bus. We had drinks and

Still Doing Things The Old Fashioned Way

sandwiches before seeing the performance of "Stanley," a three-hour play about an English artist who actually lived and who wanted to have two wives at the same time. This pièce was quite interesting to me, especially because Stanley and his artist friends would always discuss the défi (challenge) of selling works and having expositions. For most artists, this is an all important task which sometimes comes to take precedence over the actual performance of the art itself. Heaven forbid!

Many of us walked over to The Plough for a quick drink before closing, and I met several of the kids from Chapel Hill. They seemed to be just like my group that came over in 1981 which also stayed at the Haddon Hall. That was my first time abroad, and I owe thanks to Dr. Unks for encouraging me to travel by myself (my friend backed out at the last minute) through Europe after the program had ended. Then, I got a good taste, pun intended, for alternative ways of living and thinking. That's also when I got hooked on photography. Bonne nuit, Londres (Good night, London)!

A Bright Spot In The Night—Carolina Girls

London, Wednesday the 29th of May

This morning I had my English Breakfast at the other hotel with Dr. Unks, and since both hotels are of the same ownership they didn't charge me for the filling meal. We discussed a true "Traiteur" in Chapel Hill called A Southern Season and the difference in use of bright colors by southern European painters and northern European painters. The contrast is profound. Naturally, I prefer the cheery bright colors of Van Gogh's Provence to the Masterworks of Rubens and Rembrandt.

At least it's not raining! But the sky was still covered in white and gray clouds, so I took off with ASA 400 film to photograph Saint Paul's Cathedral, the second of two built on that spot since the first one was destroyed in the Great Fire of London in the late 1600s and where the Bishop of London presides. It is considered the masterpiece of architect Sir Christopher Wren who is buried there and who would not be happy about what pollution has done to this, the first domed church in the city.

Later in the afternoon, le Docteur and I had a quick lunch of sandwiches and beer and set out to do some shopping at Picadilly Circus. On the way, we stopped by the oldest French restaurant in London to reserve a table for 13h00 the following day. While walking, I enquired how my professor friend ever got started housing (at his residence) some of the great basketball players who have played for Dean Smith. He said it all started with Rusty Clark, but that he really couldn't remember the circumstances. After Rusty, there were many others such as Dick Grubar, Steve Previs, George Karl, and Mike O'Koren.

Dr. Unks wanted to find a shop that sold only shaving paraphernalia, and that, they did. The shop had every kind of brush, soap, and razor you could imagine. Only in a city like London! Anyway, I didn't buy anything, but it was interesting talking to my ex-professor of the famous Ed 41, An Introduction to Education. I'll never forget one of the things Dr. Unks emphasized over and over—"In life, you learn to do what you do and nothing else." It may sound elementary, but when it comes to fulfilling dreams, many of us are not learning how to do what we want to do.

At seven-fifteen everybody met at the Charing Cross Pier for the "Thames River Cruise" on the boat called

"The Tideways," filled with food and beverage for an evening of fun. Although I took pictures most of the time, I did get to meet some nice folks. As always, Chapel Hill has some very attractive women. After the cruise, I led a group of students to the Limelight, une boîte de nuit (a night club) in an old church. Never having gone there, I, the blind, was leading the blind. Nonetheless, I used the crude directions the kids gave me and with the good fortune I depend on, found it sans problème (without a problem). As Rainmain might have said about this disco, "It was very dark in there. Yeah, very dark." Quite right! Goodnight!

London, Thursday the 30th of May

This is the coldest May that London has had since 1659; however, today il fait chaud (it's hot). Laundry day! I washed my things in the huge English tub, and took off to see Le Musée Britanique (The British Museum). The "Lindow Man," over 2000 years old, impressed me the most of any artifact there. He was found totally intact in a bog in England in 1984. How cool! And just think, he was probably alive during the time of Jesus!

With about an hour to kill before lunch, I went hunting for the elusive perfect English-accented photograph. Well, I don't know whether or not I found it, but I did get the accent right in capturing four London telephone booths near a city market.

At noon forty-five I met the Doctor, and we proceeded to Le Mon Plaisir to dine like the French. Open since 1947, this very French adorned and appointed old house serves authentic fare. I had a Kir Royal, the légumes en salade (vegetable salad) and le panaché de poissons (variety of fish filets), un verre de vin rouge (a glass of red wine), rice, green beans, and orange sorbet with strawberries. Très déicieux! Amazingly enough, this meal cost less than it would in Paris, but don't be fooled, the cost of living here is terribly high.

This evening we saw "Sunset Boulevard" at the Adelphi Theatre after a quick meal at The Old Dutch which has been around for many years, serving huge English style crêpes and beer. My crêpe was filled with spinach, cheese, cream, and ratatouille and didn't have much flavor. The Grolshes did, however. The play was fun and full of

British Telephone Booths

action, and it helped that Dr. Unks had earlier told me the complot (the storyline). English people speaking American is almost as cool as Americans speaking with English accents. Bloody good day!

London, Paris, Lorient, vendredi 31 mai

Debout tôt (Up early)! Breakfast with Dr. Unks and then packed my bags for the adventure that awaited me. I had to get a picture of London that day, but I only had a short time before I had to leave. The British Museum offered the wonderful bronze face of a woman and that would be my only picture of the day. Around 9h30 I took a taxi to Waterloo Station where I killed some time waiting for the call for passengers traveling to France. Once inside the large waiting room, I read a magazine and watched all the people. There seemed to be hundreds waiting for the beautiful yellow engined Eurostar, truly a star in the eyes of engineers and travelers alike for its efficiency, cleanliness, tranquility, and security. If only America had trains like that!

Finally, they started calling sections (not rows like in an airplane), and soon I was in my window seat in First Class. Note: If you are planning to enjoy the onboard meal service you must be in First Class. Only snacks can be obtained in the Second Class portion of the train. At first, the train leisurely traversed the bright green countryside of Britain before stopping at la Manche (the Channel) to prepare for the underwater crossing, whatever that entails. Note: Going to Paris the meal begins at this point and by the time you're out of the Chunnel on French soil you are probably finishing your main course. Approximate crossing time is twenty minutes. I truly enjoyed the meal and the company of a couple from Chicago and an attractive English girl from Devon in the South. We had chicken in a cream sauce, vegetables, smoked salmon with a special fresh cream,

Face The Facts

bread, lots of champagne, Bordeaux wine, fruit tarts, Godiva chocolates, and coffee. We were all equally impressed with the whole experience.

Being under the English Channel reminded me of times in the métro somewhat, except in the Eurostar your ears stop up and pop from time to time due to the different altitudes, speeds, and pressures underneath the water. Naturally, everything outside of the train is pitch black, but inside there is good food and great conversation in the light of high technology. What a rush! Speaking of which, after we had stopped on the other side for routine whatever, the train flexed its muscles and got us up to 300 kilometers per hour (187MPH), skirting across the green fields of France, little houses with orange rooftops dotting the precious land of troubadours and adventuriers like myself. Believe me, it was très impressionant (very impressive) and most memorable.

I want to say we landed at La Gare du Nord, but really we just rolled in with the best of them, and I took a taxi to La Gare Montparnasse where I quickly found a chariot (luggage cart) and rushed to voie (track) #8 to catch my next train to a town called Lorient in Brittany where my friends live. Luckily, I was leaving weather that was moche (ugly), going to where there wasn't a nuage dans le ciel (cloud in the sky). Note: France is one of the most diverse countries as far as regions and topographics are concerned, and the weather can change quite rapidly from one locale to another. After the Chunnel trip and the four-and-a-half hour TGV train ride, I was ready to arrive at my destination.

Philippe was waiting for me at the station, and we drove to his home which is centrally located and full of local art.

Anne-Marie, his wife, and their son were there to greet me, and we sat around, apéros in hand, talking about art and various local peintres (painters). At ten, we ate tomatoes stuffed with tuna, lemon juice, parsley, tomato sauce, and chives—for an appetizer. It was very good and very fresh like a salad. Then we had Coquilles Saint-Jacques in a pâte feuilleté (flaky pastry shell) with some rosé wine. Strawberries with strawberry ice cream were perfect complements to our light meal.

After dinner le babysitter arrived and we drove into the country to a disco called Le Symbole. My friends had been invited to a soirée sponsored by Paco Rabanne and J&B Whisky, and at the entrance they gave us passes for free drinks. Note: Normally, you pay between 80 and 120 francs ($16-$24) just to enter a discoteque, intitling you to one consumation (drink). All other drinks will cost you $12 and up. For me, after one coup de champagne (glass of champagne) I actually fell asleep on one of the comfortable sofas. To wake up, my friend brought me a rum and fruit juice concoction which had a parallel effect. Don't let them tell you traveling is easy. I was beat. Au lit!

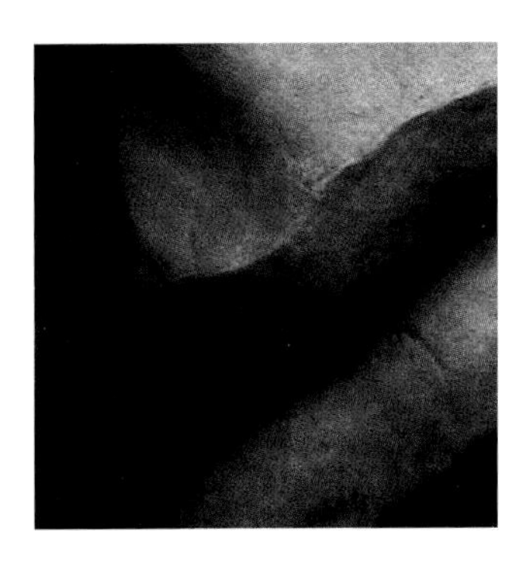

Lorient, samedi premier juin

This morning we drove to Quibéron to catch the ferry to a place I had heard so much about—Belle-Ile-En-Mer. Arnaud, their four-year-old, pestered me half way there just for fun. When we got across, a rental car was waiting for us, ready to zip up and over to La Desirade, an inn of four small pink and white villas with light blue shutters surrounding a pool. Très mignon (Very cute)!

Most of the afternoon Philippe drove me around the secluded island searching for photo opportunities. I was impressed with what I saw to say the least. There were beautiful but dangerous falaises (cliffs) that made wonderful photos and huge rock formations in the sea. There were vistas and little villages with fishermen and boats, nice Bretonne women, typical Brittany buildings, and just neat little things that only Belle-Ile-En-Mer would have.

Once again a babysitter came to take care of the "little wild man," and we took off for a place called Castel Clara high above the edge of the Atlantic. It's a restaurant that François Mitterrand used to enjoy during his most memorable visits to this wonderful bastion of eternal sea breezes. We all sat down in the comfortable bar area that looked like someone's living room and sipped on Américanos (Martini Rosso, Campari, an orange slice and a lemon slice). Then we all proceeded to order the exact same thing for dinner—des queues de langoustines avec poireaux et épinards (Dublin Bay prawn tails with leeks and spinach), and rosettes d'agneau et sa ratatouille (rare lamb medallions and its ratatouille). Dessert was stupendous! We had gratin de fruits au Sauterne which was an assortment of red and citrus fruits in a kind of sabyonne sauce made with Sauterne wine. We were very pleased with the meal, the service, and the ambience of this most attractive hotel/restaurant. But it was not over yet! Out came a plate of tempting chocolates and petits fours to accompany our Grand Marniers which left the perfect taste on the palate. The very nice gérant (manager) gave me a Grand Marnier ashtray as we were leaving to add to my collection back home. What a perfect day! Merci mes amis (Thank you, my friends)!

Cliffs And Rock Formations Of *Belle-Ile-En-Mer*

Belle-Ile-En-Mer, dimanche 2 juin

Our breakfast was served outside around the pool in the cool summer-like morning, and I especially liked the homemade preserves and pound cake. When we had gotten ready for the day, we piled in the little Peugeot 205 and headed for the sights, mostly natural wonders. Our first stop was les falaises again which are actually magnificent, dropping steeply to the sea below, eroding away with every new drop of rain. A geologist would have a field day here with all the different rock formations and the broken-off parts of cliffs in the Atlantic Ocean. What a wonder Creation can be even in destruction!

Then we returned to the inn to fetch our bicycles for use the rest of the day. This is a perfect way to see the island if the weather is nice as it was for us. Le Palais, a small village seemed to greet us as we peddled in together to have lunch at a pizzeria. We shared a large one of chèvre (goat's cheese) and merguez (spicy sausage) and Cokes. Très bon! We rode back to the inn for a short siesta and then had drinks around the pool. I heard one of Napoleon's quotes today that was quite funny, and it probably applies to me. It goes like this: "Avec les femmes la victoire est dans la fuite." (With women the victory is in the escape). And Voltaire once said, "Les femmes ressemblent aux girouettes, ...elles se fixent quand elle se rouillent." ("Women resemble weathervanes, ...they settle down when they rust.") Note: It is because I like women so much that I like to tease them.

I left the others and drove to Sauzon to photograph the little fishing village where they were unloading creeping and crawling homards (lobsters). Covering every square inch of a small village is par for a serious photographer, and I was lucky enough to find two lovely Bretonne women who allowed me to shoot their cheery faces in the sunlight of France. When I had seen everything twice, I went back to the room for un bain chaud (a hot bath).

Dinner was also in Sauzon at Café de la Cale, outside in the warm sea-scented air. We had salades vertes (green salads), crabe farcie aux crabe, champignons, crème, persil, et cétéra (crab stuffed with crabmeat, mushrooms, cream, parsley, etc.), des bigorneaux—little curli cue sea snails to pick and eat, soupe de poissons (fish soup), an assortment of goat's cheeses, and mousse au chocolat. We were stuffed, but don't say that you're plein in French. It's not poli (polite). Besides, women who are pleine are pregnant. What you say is "Je ne peux plus manger" (I can't eat any more) ou simplement (or simply), "J'ai bien mangé" (I ate well)! Dors bien (Sleep well)!

Women Of Brittany

Belle-Ile-En-Mer, lundi 3 juin

Once again we had a super petit déjeuner around the pool consisting of gateau breton (heavy buttery pound cake), a variety of confitures (preserves), all kinds of breads and viennoiserie like croissants and pain au chocolat, and un bon café très serré (a good strong coffee). Bravo! Now I can function. The very first thing I did after that wonderful breakfast was to drive to a little fishing village where I shot the bow of a boat that was only half painted in bright orange. It made a nice colorful artsy kind of cliché (photograph). Next we packed our bags, took one more look at the cliffs and drove the car back to Le Palais to catch the boat to the mainland. On dry land again, we drove to a place near Lorient called Carnac Plage, a petit village on the water. Time to eat again!

Only one restaurant was open, so we ate there. It wasn't bad. I had a salad of smoked salmon and tiny shrimp and a Poire Belle Hélène (Vanilla ice cream, pear halves, chocolate sauce, almonds, and whipped cream). When it comes to food, they do not mess around in France!

Our next stop was the art gallery-filled town of Pont Aven where I had the pleasure of meeting the well known painter, Jean Duquoc. His work is part of a movement called Nabisme, meaning he is the last painter of the style from the School of Pont Aven of which Paul Gauguin was the first. He is known as a coloriste who wants to preserve the patrimoine (pride and tradition) of Brittany on his canvases. For what seemed like hours, we had a private viewing of his work, took pictures, and drank coffee. I knew that the pastel of the sailboats was mine but wasn't sure about the oils. At the moment of truth,

Boat In *Sauzon*

when I said I was going to make a decision, I spotted a large oil of the Bigouden woman, an elderly Bretonne who used to wear the traditional clothing of the region. In a matter of minutes I was many francs poorer, and we even had to use both my Visa and Amex cards to make the purchase. It was incroyable (incredible), but I was convinced and happy with my decision.

Back in Lorient, Philippe and I were in charge of picking up groceries for dinner— saucisson dure, fromage, légumes, et cétéra. This night we ate La potée (a traditional soup full of vegetables and pork), hard dry sausages, sheep's cheese from the Pyrenées, a cheese called conté du Jura, and a wonderfully pungent blue called Forme d'Ambert. Our beverage was Côte du Rhône, a mildly spicy semi-dry red that is very often served in restos as the house wine. After dinner we discussed encore my acquisitions and then called it a night.

Alexander III Bridge

Lorient, Paris, mardi 4 juin

This morning I played with Arnaud before riding to the station to catch my train to the artful City of Light. Despite traveling at speeds of up to 187MPH, the TGV is quite comfortable and very conducive to sommeil (sleep). I indulged in a nap off and on the whole way to Paris when I wasn't listening to my baladeur (Walkman). There was a short wait for the taxi, and then I was off to 77, rue de l'Eglise where Madame was waiting excitedly to see me. She had six or seven cards and letters from the mystery woman and one from Maman (Mom). C'était dingue (It was wild)! Madame and I spoke for a bit, and she informed me that she didn't know what room I would be staying in, therefore, je n'étais pas bien organizé de tout (I was totally unorganized). Note: A seasoned traveler like myself needs to organize his affairs every time he changes locales, otherwise he feels like he may have forgotten something important like laundry or film.

I proceeded to read my courrier (mail), sitting tranquilly on the sofa, totally oblivious to the commotion around me. The mystery woman had done it again. The cards were her very own creation, brightly colored with felt tipped markers and written expressively as always. I hardly knew her, yet all the while I was beginning to fall in love with the idea of being in love. Reciprocation was in order, so I strolled over to the corner cafè for a crème and something I never do from abroad— write a real letter on letter paper. Granted, this was a long distance romance, but things seemed to be getting pretty steamy on paper. I'm not at liberty to say exactly what was written; however, from time to time my blood was rushing.

She asked me if, in a relationship, it could be fifty-fifty, and I responded, "rarement (rarely)." It's just not realistic because one of the two will always be giving up more to please the other. One of the two will always be dominant. C'est tout (That's all)! Upon my request, my postal lover sent me all of her sizes so that I might bring back some kind of fashionable gift from the birthplace of la mode (Fashion)..
On verra (We'll see)!

For the next part of my stay, I organized my city life by buying a carte orange hebdomodaire—transportation for the remainder of the week, by cashing four hundred dollars worth of travelers checks, and by posting my letter. In the late afternoon I found myself on my favorite bridge—

Pont Alexander III, and for the umpteenth time shot this merveille (wonder). Being very partial to closeups, I searched and found a beautiful but simple section of gold gilt and gray support columns. Another artsy kind of shot! Then I walked from La Madeleine to Les Champs Elysées where I dined at the Hippopotamus, a Frenchified steakhouse with food that is correcte (very acceptable). I started with a Kir Royal, then a glass of Saint Emilion with my filet mignon de margret de canard (duck medallions) with béarnaise sauce and French green beans. I took my coffee at the attractive bar from the attractive bartender and left very satisfied.

The Poker Player

Paris, mercredi 5 juin

After a typical morning, I rode the buses to the Terminus of #43 where I found a well known Traiteur called Hédiard which makes some delicious things to take away and eat at home, or like me, for a pique-nique in the park. I selected une tranche (a slice) of the terrine de légumes (vegetable pâté) with leeks, broccoli, carrots, and hearts of artichokes with a bland tasting tomato sauce. The pâté en croute (meat terrine in pastry) looked good, so I ordered a slice of that and an Orangina to drink with my gourmet lunch in the grandeur nature (wide open).

Once inside the Parc de Bagatelle, I found a nice bench in one of the many gardens and ate royally. This civilized food sure beats a sandwich. When I had thoroughly enjoyed my meal, I began to photograph what was around me including La Roseraie (The Rose Garden). C'était si beau et si jolie (It was so beautiful and so nice)!

The French never cease to amaze me. Today I got a picture of the owner of an antique store playing poker with a friend outside of his shop during lunchtime. This is part of what the stereotyped lifestyle is all about here in wonderful France.

Wouldn't you know that I would end up at my favorite célèbre salon de thé (famous tea room) around five—Ladurée! And I truly enjoyed the light nothing dessert they prepared for me of meringue, fresh chantilly cream, and perfect framboises (raspberries). Now that is what a dessert should be—light, airy, fluffy, fresh, creamy, sweet, and simple. The French often describe their cooking as simple mais bon (simple but good). My Thé Ceylan Devonia with milk was the perfect beverage to wash down the sweet fruity fluff of air which was ideal because it wasn't so much that it took away my appetite for dinner.

Ladurée is so beautiful and well appointed inside with chairs and tables of wood with inlaid marble tops, each one having a brass number, possibly more for looks than to help the very friendly waitresses keep up with their customers. Speaking of the serveuses (waitresses), they are nicely dressed in traditional black dresses with white collars. The windows, although they do let light in are not very significant, however, the Bordeaux, gray, and blue colors play an important role in the overall welcoming ambience. The walls are in mirror and gold with very elaborate paintings that are the same colors as the tapis (rug). The ceiling is a painting of the blue sky with clouds and des anges (angels) in the middle, illuminated by a forte lumière (strong light). Extrêmement jolie (Extremely beautiful)! Note: As soon as you enter this establishment many of the pâtisseries and desserts will be on display to your left. If you must, tell the waitress that you will show her which one you desire, otherwise, you may have a problem with the menu names of many of the délices (delights).

After reading my magazine called "PHOTO" with an interesting story on Liv Tyler, I ducked in the Le Royal Tour, a bar/brasserie where I had a simple salade composée (mixed salad) and a Coke, all for under ten dollars. Normale! I couldn't help but think about my penpal "friend" in the US. She's on fire! And I'm intrigued by the attention and her creativity, but, Geez, we've only known each other for two months and one of those I've spent here in France. On verra (We'll see)!

Place Des Vosges

Paris, jeudi 6 juin

Le Marais is quite possibly the new "most happening neighborhood" in Paris, and on this hot day I went there to photograph les environs (the area). There you will find many reasonably priced restaurants, cute shops, and a nice community of Jewish people. My favorite place, as it is for most folks, is La Place des Vosges, a large rectangular courtyard with old trees lining the four sides and dirt footpaths with a garden park in the middle and a beautiful brick building of mansions and small flats that housed royalty in the nineteenth siècle (century). "La Place" is old. It was begun in 1605 and inaugurated in 1612 by Henry IV, and tourists love to meander and sit in the French garden.

Alors (well), I had worked up an appetite, so I found a vieux resto (old restaurant) called Le Guirlande de Julie which means The Wreath or Garland of Julie. Its located at #25 under the arcades of La Place, and you must not miss it if you happen to be there for a meal. The service is good and the waiters are friendly, not to mention the delicious cuisine. I started with an apéro de pinot de Charentes and then a cup of very fresh Gaspacho which inspired me to create some when I got home to the states again. My plat principal (main course) was what has become my signature dish— margret de canard signant avec des poires en tranches (sliced medium rare rotisserie duck breast with pear slices). Dessert was short and sweet—three sorbets of exotic fruits and a café. L'addition, s'il vous plaît (The bill please)!

Later, as I was standing before the Hôtel du Crillon, a Mercedes pulled up and the mec (guy) driving asked me how to get to le parking for the Place de la Concorde, and I instinctively turned and saw the sign and pointed it out to this lost traveler. When he had driven off, a bit shocked that I was able to help him, I realized that I had behaved much like the French would in similar circumstances. You see, when you ask for directions, the French will always at least get you to the next person from whom to ask directions. For example, they might say, "Go two blocks and ask again" because even if they haven't the slightest idea, they will send you somewhere. As for me, I got lucky, but at least I didn't say that I wasn't from there and therefore had no idea. I now consider myself a local and no longer a tourist. I passed the test.

Just as he had requested back in the States, I called Bruce at the Hilton, and he was sleeping from the day's flight over. He just arrived this morning from Wilmington and was surprised to hear from me. We made a plan to meet and have dinner at my new favorite place at eight-thirty. Note: When it gets as hot as it was today you really need to shower and change clothes before dinner. So I did, and then descended from Bir Hakim, the mètro stop nearest the Eiffel Tower, and walked to the Hilton bar where Bruce and I had drinks with the sportscasters and tennis greats Cliff Dreysdale and Fred Stolle, who were in town for Roland Garros (The French Open). Then it was on to rue Monttessuy where the fabulous 100 percent French restaurant called Au Bon Acceuil is found. We dined like kings with these two celebs. Fred, one of the funniest people around, entertained us. Unusually, I imbibed a little Côte du Rhône Blanc, and it wasn't bad for a white. I had La Rondelle de Poireaux aux quenelles de saumon (baby leeks with salmon pâté), pan sautéed merlan (a small fish) aux sauce de tomates (in tomato sauce), profiteroles au chocolat and that's it. Cliff, Fred, and Bruce were as content as I was with the excellent repas (meal) which came to a reasonable price. Pas mal (not bad)!

Paris, vendredi 7 juin

Bruce telephoned this morning to let me know that he would be attending the women's finals and the men's semi-finals at Roland Garros. Quelle chance (What luck)! France really gets excited about this sporting event, and everyone seems to have it on their minds, especially here in Paris. Since I had business to attend to myself and since I didn't have a ticket for the tennis, I didn't tempt the fate of being scalped by going to Le Bois de Bologne (The Bologne Woods) where the stade (stadium) is found.

I spoke to the lady doing my show, and she gave me the go-ahead to send her my selection of slides of Paris. After that bit of good news, my mind started racing about all the little details I had to work out to pull this thing off. Should I have my work framed and then sent to France, or should I bring the prints over in the plane and have them framed here. Like all important decisions, the answer will become clear over time. At some point I will have to design and create une affiche (a poster) for the show with one of my best photos and my name underneath. A CV (Curriculum Vitae or resume) will also be necessary. Instead of inches, I had to think en centimetres for the size of photos, frames, and mats, so I figured 2.54 centimeters per inch and calculated the sizes from that.

My afternoon was spent taking pictures after visiting a traiteur and picnicking on terrine de homard et sa sauce rosé (lobster terrine and its pink sauce), baked endives, and a pizza without cheese [drôle (funny)]. Once again I found myself at one of my favorite places to shoot pictures—Le Pont Alexander III. This time I captured the bronze face of a beautiful statue of a child.

Newly Restored Bronze On The Alexander III Bridge

Around seven thirty I met Bruce and we caught a cab without climatization (air conditioning) which could have been worse had it been any warmer. Plus, we had our windows open the whole way. Our destination was 71, rue de Caulaincourt in the dix-huitième (eighteenth arrondissement) up near Montmartre where we dined with Astride and Philippe, a very nice couple who have a four-year-old son. After un verre de Pinot d'Alsace, a light fruity white from Astrid's family vineyard, we climbed the hill to a resto near Le Sacré Coeur (Sacred Heart Church). Au Clocher de Montmartre, with its cuisine from the region of Auvergne in the center of France, it was bustling with activity. It was already late and they had run out of some of their entrées, so I had a salad with blue cheese dressing, grilled pork chops, and pommes frites (French fries). Très correcte! On s'est bien amusé (We had a great time)! Le Fleurie we drank first was not a good bottle of wine; however, Le Beaune après was extraordinaire. English was the language of choice for the evening because Astrid, who makes her living translating books, speaks quite fluently.

After yet another substantial and delicious French meal we strolled to and around the basilica which is very animé (animated) at night with tourists everywhere, Africans selling their wares, and snack vendors. Our next stop was La Place du Tertre, where crowds move about the artists with there easels and canvases inside the energizing square and gather in the many café/restaurants for a meal or just a refreshing beer. At minuit (midnight) we returned to their apartment for more photos and some eau de vie (strong fruit brandy) made by Astrid's brother. Another day in the life of Paris!

Paris, samedi 8 juin

This morning my only clean button-down needed a bouton and low and behold Madame found one that matched perfectly, so for the first time in twenty years I sewed on a button. While I performed my task we talked about how artists have been and are often still exclus de la société (excluded from society), meaning that they somehow don't quite fit in with the "in" crowd. There was even a time when artists were treated as low class laborers in the court of a King. Today, artists seem to be more respected and freer to create whatever their imaginations dictate; however, even material success does not equal social acceptance. Most artists are very different in the way they think and in the way they communicate with others. Madame showed me how the cinema has helped the artist gain acceptance in society, but well before Van Gogh, "unsuccessful" creatives were never graciously received by the public. Ironically, they are often the ones who travel further into the vast imagination of man to show humanity a clearer picture of itself in masterpiece after masterpiece. We both agreed; however, that adversity has very often come to be the artist's best friend. Etrange, non (Isn't it strange)?

Bruce called and wanted me to reserve a table for six at Au Bon Acceuil, but they were booked solid, so I decided to try Le Grand Colbert, a grand restaurant from the Belle Epoque which naturally has good food. I called, and we were in. I went to the Trocadéro and took some pix of the people skating and jumping like acrobats and the Eiffel Tower in all its glory. You know, it's funny because you can be almost anywhere in the city and look up and see the top of that French phallic

It Is Very Difficult To Hide A 300-Meter Tower

symbol peaking over any old building. Speaking of which, Guy de Maupassant, a great French writer in the late 1800s once said of this massive metal structure, "It's the only place I can go in Paris where I don't have to see it." Some things will always be controversial for the French. They wouldn't have it any other way. Hey, even an argument to Americans is a civilized conversation to the French.

After my cheapest beer ever in Paris at the 3 Ducks Hostel, a haven for young travelers on strict budgets, I metroed it to La Bourse, the Wallstreet Stock Exchange of France. I arrived early and enjoyed a Kir Royal while I waited. Shortly thereafter Bruce, Cliff, and his friend Julie, une jolie fille de Boston (an attractive woman from Boston) arrived and ordered what I was having. Although the resto wasn't bustling we all agreed that it was quite good. I had des fonds d'artichauts frais (fresh artichoke hearts) in a mustard vinaigrette, turbot grillé avec une sauce Béarnaise (grilled turbot with a béarnaise sauce), fondant de chocolat sauce anglaise avec zests de mandarine (pâté of chocolate in a sweet cream with crystallized mandarine peels), and a décaf. Ultra bon!

Totally satisfied, we all left Le Grand Colbert with a glow on our faces that only good food and wine can produce. My friends caught a taxi and I chose to walk it off a little by heading to La Concorde where I took the métro to Felix Faure and walked home. Voilà (There you have it)!

Paris, dimanche 9 juin

J'ai fait la grasse matinée (I slept in) and took my "traveling companion" to a café called A La Tour Eiffel devant l'église (in front of the church). Not uncommonly, we wandered around from quartier to quartier looking for something interesting to shoot. And also not uncommonly, we found ourselves in the Saint-Germain des Près area where we had Sunday lunch on the sidewalk at Le Muniche—an assortment of margret de canard, cuisses de canard, champignons, et salade (Sliced duck breast, leg of duck, mushrooms, and salad). The Kir was offert (free) and the fresh orange juice was a pleasant surprise because I hadn't had any in so long. Voilà! C'était bon (It was good)! Note: In France restaurants often have outdoor seating almost year round, even if it's under an umbrella and a heater on a narrow sidewalk. Although weather does not always permit, restaurant goers dine outside whenever possible, because the climate in this blessed country lends itself to eating under open skies, that is, little humidity and few bêtes (flies).

I later photographed Le Pont des Arts, a wood and metal pedestrian bridge where artists like to create or just hang out. I found out almost the hard way that vélos (bicycles) are allowed over the expanse when a young lady almost ran over me while I was shooting this amusingly dressed man and the Institut de France behind him. It never crossed her mind to slow down or even stop. Note: Just like in America, you don't need a license to ride a bike in France. I was a little perturbed, nevertheless, at that very moment I took my photograph. When I crossed over to La Rive Gauche (The Left Bank) where sits the old Institut De France, home of the Academie Française as well as other vital French institutions, I

Interesting Local With *Rafraîchissment*

proceeded along the river until I had reached my favorite museum in France— Le Musée d'Orsay which houses some of the finest Impressionist works in mankind's possession. Being so close to my favorite bridge in Paris, I had to stop by the Alexander III to catch a few more clichés of the beauty of the Ville de Paris.

At 18h00 I met Bruce at the Hôtel La Concorde Lafayette which is un veritable gratte-en-ciel (a veritable sky scraper) that stands many stories tall at Port Maillot and the inner périphérique (beltway). For a change of pace and because it was so hot outside we had some cokas (Coke) with plenty of ice cubes and a lemon slice. Vraiment rafraichîssant (Truly refreshing)! Then we went to my friend Jeanne-Marie's flat nearby to have a cocktail and I took pictures of her and her lifelong friend who loves to speak English. Note: Jeanne-Marie is part of the family I lived with when I created my first photo journal. Vers neuf heures (Around nine o'clock) we headed to one of their favorite wine bars called La Verre en Bouteille at the foot of avenue des Ternes. I ordered the wine which was a medium dry red that didn't cost an arm and a leg, and we all got along swell, although Jeanne-Marie, like many of my French friends, enjoys giving me a hard time about what I do for a living. And of note, tomorrow Bruce would experience the TGV (Train à Grande Vitesse) for the first time en route to Avignon. I had a salad with blue cheese dressing, le panaché de poissons (tuna and salmon in a light sauce), and un gâteau au chocolat mi-cuit avec sa sauce anglaise (half-cooked chocolate cake in a sweet vanilla cream sauce). Très délicieux! Salut!

Phantoms In the Moonlight Of *Rue De Lappe*

Paris, lundi 10 juin

Before I took my café au café (coffee at a coffee house) I shot the beautiful Opéra Garnier with a telephoto lens and I believe I captured what I wanted in a perfect horizon which is hard to do without a trépied (tripod). Then Guy and Catherine called to let me know we were to meet at the café Royal Opéra. The place was bustling and we wanted something a little more laid back, so we walked to the nearby Jardin des Tuilleries (Tuillerie Gardens in front of the Louvre museum) where we enjoyed having lunch in the garden under an umbrella. All of us had work to do later, so we ate light-salads, coka pour moi (Coke for me), wine for Guy and Catherine, delightful pêches melbas (peaches, vanilla ice cream and raspberry coulis) to compliment the springtime meal, and coffee. Guy loves to give me a hard time about what I do for a living. To him, my trips to France are *cent pourcent* (100 percent) vacation time. He always asks me what I'm going to do when I return to the United States, even though he already knows that I'm a photographer and a writer. *Au revoir, mes amis, et à la prochaine* (Bye-bye, my friends, until next time)!

After lunch I headed to the Montparnasse train station from which I walked along *L'Avenue du Maine* to an *encadreur* (picture framer) suggested to me weeks ago by the nice man in the art *galerie* off *rue Saint Honoré*. Once I had explained to the gentlemen of *Claude CORSI* that I would need twelve large photos matted and framed, they offered me a beer—*très français* (very French)! Note: Shops all over Paris have refrigerators with beer and/or *champagne* expressly for the purpose of entertaining potential big spenders, and it works. You cannot imagine how welcome you feel when nice people offer you a drink in the middle of the day while you are shopping in a foreign land. All of a sudden, shopping becomes a party, and usually Visa and Amex are invited. The CORSI brothers' father used to do the framing years ago, and now it's them and an assistant. They do excellent work and at a price I can live with. Once we were clear on all of the dimensions and details for the work, I left the shop feeling good about my show in September.

After a sprint over to *Les Halles* and one of my favorite shops—*Chistera*, I bought a nice plant for *Madame. Elle était très contente* (She was quite pleased) and thanked me for the lovely gift. We then chatted for a while, and she showed me the beautiful sculptures created by her *fille* (daughter). We seem to get into these philosophical conversations that go all over and end up with a kind of universal, "Well, I really don't know, but for some/most people this is how it is." Today we decided that everyone has either the capacity to appreciate art, to perform it or both. Profond (Profound)! It began to rain, so I got mon impérméable (my raincoat) and walked to an Au Poivrier!, one of a chain of reasonable restos in Paris, where I indulged in a fancy rum cocktail, saumon fumé sur toast beurré (smoked salmon on buttered toast), salade des grissons (salad with a special kind of sliced meat from the Alps), a glass of Saint-Emilion, and a décaf. Très correcte!

The sky cleared and the moon came out about the time I arrived at the Bastille Métro Station. From there I walked past the new Opera House and the crowded restos to an up and coming quartier, most notably, the Rue de Lappe. This nocturnally crowded, narrow street is where one finds all sorts of Tapas Bars and various other watering holes for a good stiff drink or a glass of red Spanish wine. There are places to dance, however, my mission was clear—shoot the nightlife!

Expensive Office Space Of The *Grand Arch De La Défense*

Paris, mardi 11 juin

Since it was my last morning in France, I spoiled myself with an almond croissant, the richest most delectable breakfast pastry I know of. My crème washed it down well and got me revved up to pack my bags for the long-three leg journey home. It was still early enough to rush over to La Défense which is a super-modern downtown of skyscrapers and a beautiful white arch positioned in a perfect line with its older brother, L'Arc de Triomphe. This huge arch has offices on both sides and I shot them from the sunny side and got a modern vision of Paris.

Madame called a cab for me, and around ten I was headed to Aérogare #1 where USAirways flies out of. In the very tempting duty-free areas I try not to load myself down, but I did promise my brother some foie gras de canard (duck liver), so I hunted that down before boarding the plane which was full to the brim.

I sat beside a college student who didn't have as much to say as he did to drink. He just kept ordering bourbon and Coke with an occasional Bailey's Irish Cream. Yuk! The meal was correcte— salamis, cheese, rolls, grilled salmon, spinach, rice, Glen Ellen cabernet sauvignon, fruit, and a lemon tart. Although uneventful flights are pleasant, I would have preferred sitting next to a beautiful young blond or even a brunette. Oh well, maybe on my next trip! À bientôt j'espère (Hope to see you soon)!

After experiencing this journal, do you wonder why France is the number one tourist destination in the world? When I think of France, I think of a song by Phil Collins that sings of a woman who has a special attraction that you cannot resist. Yet the attraction is not just "invisible" or "physical." It is visual. It is sensual. And it is spiritual. No one goes there and comes home without a strong opinion about her. It is never *comme ci, comme ça* (so-so). People either fall in love again in France, or she pisses them off for a myriad of reasons. Those who are not content with her have usually not spent much time there and have probably had some bad luck which could have been because of poor preparation and planning. Whatever the reason may be, a significant majority return and return religiously because they have found something that truly stimulates their love for living life to the fullest. Sure, I am speaking for myself here, too, but many would agree.

In 1983 I lived with a family in *Vichy* who used to serve me apple everything— apple tarts, apple pie, baked apples, apple fritters, apple *soufflé*, apple sauce, stewed apples, apples, and I couldn't figure it out. All I knew was that I was losing weight eating apples all the time. I thought the family was somewhat poor because the husband was a house painter, the grandfather lived in the house, and the attic was full of rent-paying nursing students. Everyday, I would walk a mile and a half to class and a mile and a half home twice, once each day for lunch with apples and then in the late afternoon as well. Yes, I am exaggerating a bit, because *Madame* really made some healthy *purée* of vegetable soups and tasty sausages, too. Anyway, at this time in my life I didn't drink much wine, so when offered *un verre* (a glass) I would graciously decline. *Le Monsieur*, however, would fill his glass with one quarter wine and three quarters water and drink it with dinner. The wine was bulk table wine, for little more than a few *francs* per glass. Why, I wondered, did the French girls not eat with us? Meals were a little *triste* (sad), because all we could do was look at each other. My French was horrible, if nonexistent, at the time.

One day I was scolded for taking two showers. One was the limit, because in this, the City of Water, *l'eau chaude est chère* (the hot water is expensive). The whole time I was living there, I did not realize that the adjoining house was also theirs, that *Monsieur* and *Madame* never slept in the house, that they had a country house nearby with, what else, an apple orchard, and that their daughter was a successful businesswoman in Paris. This was my first experience with this French mentality. Later I discovered that there are those who have little but act like they have a lot, and there are those who have it all and act like they have nothing.

My true love affair with France began after two months of study at CAVILAM when my friend, *Philippe*, introduced me to the music of *Francis Cabrel*, which speaks so fluently about people and life in general. Although I could, I will not compare him to our James Taylor or Jackson Brown at this time. The youthful *Cabrel* from the *Carcassone* region of France captures a culture in resonant lyrical tunes which entertain and speak to the heart. I was particularly moved by the song *Les Chevaliers Cathares* which speaks of the irony and absurdity of a monument, built by the extended central power that eradicated the Cathar

Street Performer

sect because of its threat to Catholicism many years ago. Ironically, it sadly stands at *une aire* (a rest stop) along the *autoroute* which used to be *champs de torture* (fields of torture) for the Cathar monks. "The Chevalier Cathares cry softly, on the side of the freeway when the nightime falls...Like a last insult, like a final torment, in the middle of the tumult, enrobed in cement" are just some of the evocative words translated into English. His songs are thoughtful, the words often hauntingly truthful, and he continues to sell out large venues all over the *Hexagone*. Only some of his songs will bring you to tears, but his greatest love song to date has to be, *"Je t'aimais, Je t'aime, et Je t'aimerai* (I loved you, I love you, and I will love you," which sounds much better *en français*. I could go on and on, but I just wanted to express how important cultural aspects of a country such as its poetry, can win your heart and open a whole new world of discovery. Besides, music has always helped me to identify with the people and places in my life. Of all the things which attract me to a culture, there is an unidentifiable, invisible power which resonates in my musical mind. That is what I miss most when I am not in France. *Alors*, for me, before the good food, the photogenic sites, and the rich history, there was *Francis Cabrel* and his unique expression of this, a most expressive language.

I remember the evening in *Vichy* when I began to realize that food was synonymous with France. My friend Tom was living *chez Madame Bonnefoy*, and she invited me to dine with her household of *locataires* (boarders). We started with *Kirs*, and *amuse-gueules*, then a sumptuous rabbit stew with potatoes, carrots, and onions, and *une salad verte* with that tantalizing mustard vinaigrette that almost always dresses French salads. *Madame B.* puts fresh *ail* (garlic) in her sauce to make it extra flavorful. We drank a light *Beaujolais* with the meal because one of the students had visited the region recently and had brought back several bottles. Dessert was chocolate mousse on *genoise* (sponge cake) topped with *chantilly* cream, and we even had a little *champagne* with it. *Très français* (Very French)! I believe it's the rhythm of a French meal that makes it truly *français*, but the delightful flavors and palate quenching beverages help create a truly memorable experience.

Rudolf, a Russian stomach doctor, was my first friend from class, and we would often try to communicate in very broken French. Neither one of us had ever seen the likes of, for him, an American and for me, a Russian. We had *tellement de questions* to ask each other, and this helped motivate me to learn. What also helped was my desire to express myself, talk about my home, meet new people, and quite simply, pick up chicks. Hey, I was 23 at the time. I believe I had a slight crush on my teacher, who looked a lot like Stevie Nicks and who was just divorced, but it wasn't in the cards for me to have "French lessons" after class. Soon I began my love affair with the *langue* (language), and the rest is history.

It was about this time when I met the beautiful *Jacqueline*, but unfortunately that journal was stolen in The Great Paris BMW Heist of 1984, and I cannot remember a thing, yet! Who knows, one bright day could bring it all back to me and I'd have to write *toute l'histoire* (The Whole Story). *Restez branché* (Stay tuned)!